Best Easy Day Hikes Series

Best Easy Day Hikes
Richmond, Virginia

Johnny Molloy

FALCONGUIDES

GUILFORD, CONNECTICUT
HELENA, MONTANA

AN IMPRINT OF GLOBE PEQUOT PRESS

FALCONGUIDES®

Maps by Off Route Inc. © Morris Book Publishing, LLC

Library of Congress Cataloging-in-Publication Data
Molloy, Johnny, 1961-
  Best easy day hikes, Richmond, Virginia / Johnny Molloy.
      p. cm. – (Falconguides)
  ISBN 978-0-7627-5850-0
  1. Hiking–Virginia–Richmond Region–Guidebooks. 2. Trails–Virginia–Richmond Region–Guidebooks. 3. Richmond Region (Va.)–Guidebooks. I. Title.
  GV199.42.V8M65 2010
  796.5109755'451–dc22
                              2009043061

Printed in the United States of America

10 9 8 7 6 5 4 3 2 1

Contents

The Hikes

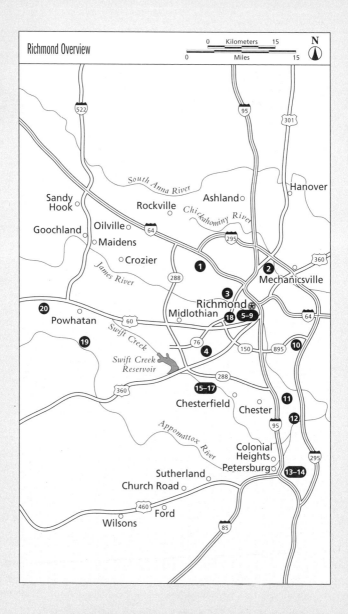

Richmond Overview

Acknowledgments

Thanks to all the people who helped me with this book, especially Pamela Morgan. Thanks to Nathan Burrell, coordinator of Richmond's trails, to Jim Hunt and Lightfoot, too. Also, thanks to all the park personnel who answered my tireless questions while trying to manage these jewels of the Old Dominion. The biggest thanks go to the hikers of Richmond and the greater capital area, for without y'all the trails wouldn't be there in the first place.

Introduction

The gray boulder on Belle Isle sat perilously close to raucous rapids of the James River. I stood atop the rock looking northward across the water, toward downtown. The outspread landscape contained parts of James River Park, the location of many hikes in this book. My mind soared beyond downtown while mentally recounting all the scenic hikes of greater Richmond. Nearby, Gregory's Pond lay silent beside the wooded trails of Rockwood Park. To the east the fountain of Dorey Lake greeted hikers. To the north the green oasis of Deep Run Park shaded walking paths used by daily exercisers, while Three Lakes Park contained a watery trailside getaway. To the south stood the large jewel of Pocahontas State Park, where natural beauty overlain with the historic Civilian Conservation Corps past made the trail system a delight, demanding multiple hikes for inclusion in this book. Dutch Gap Conservation Area was laced with miles of alluring trails and a chance to visit a re-created English village from the 1600s. Dodd Park offered bluffside hiking along the Appomattox River and a fascinating boardwalk over Ashton Creek Marsh. The hikes at Petersburg National Battlefield explored Civil War history amid rolling hills divided by quiet streams. Other destinations were developed purely with recreation in mind. Hikers and mountain bikers enjoyed a network of hillside paths. I scanned west to Powhatan and Amelia wildlife management areas, where Richmond residents can enjoy rural walks in large preserved areas, maybe to spot a deer or wild turkey.

With this book in hand—and willing feet—you can explore the greater Richmond region. No matter where you go, the trails in this book will enhance your outdoor experience and leave you appreciating the natural splendors of the greater capital area. Enjoy.

The Nature of Richmond and the Greater Capital Region

Richmond's hiking grounds range from single-track wooded trails along bountiful lakes and streams to flat and paved downtown strolls. Hikes in this guide cover the gamut. While by definition a best easy day hike is not strenuous and generally poses little danger to the traveler, knowing a few details about the nature of greater Richmond will enhance your explorations.

Weather

Richmond certainly experiences all four seasons. Summer can be warm, with occasional downright hot spells, and is the least popular hiking season. Thunderstorms can pop up in the afternoons. I recommend hiking during the early morning or late in the evening in summer. Hiking increases when the first northerly fronts of fall sweep cool, clear air across central Virginia. Crisp mornings give way to warm afternoons. Fall is drier than summer and is the driest of all seasons. Winter will bring frigid subfreezing days and chilling rains, even snow. However, a brisk hiking pace will keep you warm. Each cold month has several days of mild weather. Spring will be more variable. A warm day can be followed by a cold one. Extensive spring rains bring regrowth but also keep hikers indoors. But any avid hiker will find more good hiking days than they will have time to hike in spring and every other season.

Critters

Richmond trail treaders will encounter mostly benign creatures on these trails, such as deer, squirrels, rabbits, wild turkeys, and a variety of songbirds. More rarely seen (during the daylight hours especially) are coyotes, raccoons, and opossums. Deer in some of the parks are remarkably tame and may linger on or close to the trail as you approach. If you feel uncomfortable when encountering any critter, keep your distance and they will generally keep theirs.

Be Prepared

Hiking in greater Richmond is generally safe. Still, hikers should be prepared, whether they are out for a short stroll at James River Park or venturing into the secluded Powhatan Wildlife Management Area. Some specific advice:

- Know the basics of first aid, including how to treat bleeding, bites and stings, and fractures, strains, or sprains. Pack a first-aid kit on each excursion.

- Familiarize yourself with the symptoms of heat exhaustion and heat stroke. Heat exhaustion symptoms include heavy sweating, muscle cramps, headache, dizziness, and fainting. Should you or any of your hiking party exhibit any of these symptoms, cool the victim down immediately by rehydrating and getting him or her to an air-conditioned location. Cold showers also help reduce body temperature. Heat stroke is much more serious: The victim may lose consciousness and the skin is hot and dry to the touch. In this event, call 911 immediately.

- Regardless of the weather, your body needs a lot of water while hiking. A full 32-ounce bottle is the minimum for these short hikes, but more is always better. Bring a full water bottle, whether water is available along the trail or not.

- Don't drink from streams, rivers, creeks, or lakes without treating or filtering the water first. Waterways and water bodies may host a variety of contaminants, including giardia, which can cause serious intestinal unrest.

- Prepare for extremes of both heat and cold by dressing in layers.

- Carry a backpack in which you can store extra clothing, ample drinking water and food, and whatever goodies, like guidebooks, cameras, and binoculars, you might want. Consider bringing a GPS equipped with tracking capabilities.

- Most Richmond trails have cell phone coverage. Bring your device, but make sure you've turned it off or got it on the vibrate setting while hiking. Nothing like a "wake the dead"-loud ring to startle every creature, including fellow hikers.

- Keep children under careful watch. Trails travel along many rivers, streams, and lakes, which are not recommended for swimming. Hazards along some of the trails include poison ivy, uneven footing, and steep dropoffs; make sure children don't stray from the designated route. Children should carry a plastic whistle; if they become lost, they should stay in one place and blow the whistle to summon help.

Zero Impact

Trails in Richmond and neighboring communities are well used year-round, especially the trails of James River Park.

We, as trail users, must be especially vigilant to make sure our passage leaves no lasting mark. Here are some basic guidelines for preserving trails in the region:

- Pack out all your own trash, including biodegradable items like orange peels. You might also pack out garbage left by less considerate hikers.
- Don't approach or feed any wild creatures—the ground squirrel eyeing your snack food is best able to survive if it remains self-reliant.
- Don't pick wildflowers or gather rocks, antlers, feathers, and other treasures along the trail. Removing these items will only take away from the next hiker's experience.
- Avoid damaging trailside soils and plants by remaining on the established route. This is also a good rule of thumb for avoiding poison ivy and stinging nettle, common regional trailside irritants.
- Be courteous by not making loud noises while hiking.
- Many of these trails are multiuse, which means you'll share them with other hikers, trail runners, mountain bikers, and equestrians. Familiarize yourself with the proper trail etiquette, and be sure to yield the trail when appropriate.
- Use outhouses at trailheads or along the trail.

Richmond Area Boundaries and Corridors

For the purposes of this guide, best easy day hikes are confined to a one-hour drive from downtown Richmond. The hikes reach into Petersburg and the counties of Chesterfield, Henrico, Prince George, Amelia, and Powhatan.

A number of major highways and interstates converge in Richmond. Directions to trailheads are given from these arteries. They include I-95, I-295, I-895, I-64, Powhite Parkway, and Chippenham Parkway.

Land Management

The following government organizations manage most of the public lands described in this guide and can provide further information on these hikes and other trails in their service areas.

- Virginia State Parks, 203 Governor St., Suite 302, Richmond, VA 23219-2094; (800) 933-PARK; www .dcr.virginia.gov/state_parks/

- Richmond Department of Parks, Recreation and Community Facilities, 900 East Broad St., Richmond, VA 23219; (804) 646-7000; www.richmondgov.com/ departments/parks/

- Chesterfield County Parks and Recreation, 9901 Lori Rd., Chesterfield, VA 23832-0040; (804) 748-1623; www.chesterfield.gov

- Henrico County Division of Recreation & Parks, P.O. Box 90775, Henrico, VA 23273-0775; (804) 501-7275; www.co.henrico.va.us/rec/

How to Use This Book

This guide is designed to be simple and easy to use. Each hike is described with a map and summary information that delivers the trail's vital statistics including length, difficulty, fees and permits, park hours, canine compatibility, and trail contacts. Directions to the trailhead are also provided, along with a general description of what you'll see along the way. A detailed route finder (Miles and Directions) sets forth mileages between significant landmarks along the trail.

Hike Selection

This guide describes trails that are accessible to every hiker, whether visiting from out of town or someone lucky enough to live in greater Richmond. The hikes are no longer than 7 miles round-trip, and most are considerably shorter. They range in difficulty from flat excursions perfect for a family outing to more challenging hilly treks. While these trails are among the best, keep in mind that nearby trails, often in the same park or preserve, may offer options better suited to your needs. I've sought to space hikes throughout the greater capital region, so wherever your starting point, you'll find a great easy day hike nearby.

Difficulty Ratings

These are all easy hikes, but easy is a relative term. To aid in the selection of a hike that suits particular needs and abilities, each is rated easy, moderate, or more challenging. Bear in mind that even more challenging routes can be made easy by hiking within your limits and taking rests when you need them.

- **Easy** hikes are generally short and flat, taking no longer than an hour to complete.
- **Moderate** hikes involve increased distance and relatively mild changes in elevation and will take one to two hours to complete.
- **More challenging** hikes feature some steep stretches, greater distances, and generally take longer than two hours to complete.

These are completely subjective ratings—consider that what you think is easy is entirely dependent on your level of fitness and the adequacy of your gear (primarily shoes). If you are hiking with a group, you should select a hike with a rating that's appropriate for the least fit and prepared in your party.

Approximate hiking times are based on the assumption that on flat ground, most walkers average 2 miles per hour. Adjust that rate by the steepness of the terrain and your level of fitness (subtract time if you're an aerobic animal and add time if you're hiking with kids), and you have a ballpark hiking duration. Be sure to add more time if you plan to picnic or take part in other activities like bird-watching or photography.

Trail Finder

Best Hikes for River and Stream Lovers

Best Hikes for Lake Lovers

Best Hikes for Children

Best Hikes for Dogs

Best Hikes for Great Views

Best Hikes for Nature Lovers

Best Hikes for History Buffs

Map Legend

═══⟨8⟩═══	Interstate Highway
═══⟨19⟩═══	U.S. Highway
═══⟨34⟩═══	State Highway
═══════	Local Road
▬ ▬ ▬ ▬ ▬	Featured Trail
- - - - - -	Trail
─────────	Paved Trail
⊢─┼─┼─┼─┤	Railroad
～～～～	River/Creek
—·—·—·—	Intermittent Stream
◯	Lake
	Marsh
⦀⦀⦀	Boardwalk
⏝	Bridge
⋀	Camping
•─•	Gate
❓	Information Center
🅿	Parking
🔳	Picnic Area
■	Point of Interest/Structure
🔳	Ranger Station
∬	Rapids
🔳	Restroom
🗼	Tower
○	Town
⓫	Trailhead
🔳	Viewpoint/Overlook
⟲	Spring

1 Deep Run Park Hike

This hike takes you on a couple of the many short trails in Deep Run Park, including the quieter north end of the retreat. The paved path wanders through hickory–oak woods and near developed facilities before backtracking. A trip to Deep Run will lure you to return and explore the rest of the well-kept paths that draw in nearby residents for their daily exercise.

Distance: 1.9 miles out and back with a short loop
Approximate hiking time: 1 to 1.6 hours
Difficulty: Easy
Trail surface: Asphalt
Best season: Year-round
Other trail users: Joggers, bicyclists
Canine compatibility: Leashed dogs permitted
Fees and permits: No fees or permits required
Schedule: Dawn to dusk
Maps: Deep Run Park map; USGS map: Glen Allen
Trail contacts: Deep Run Park, 9900 Ridgefield Parkway, Richmond, 23233 (804) 501-7275; www.co.henrico.va.us/rec/parks

Finding the trailhead: From exit 180A on I-64 northwest of downtown Richmond, take Gaskins Road south for 0.9 mile, then turn right onto Ridgefield Parkway. Follow Ridgefield Parkway 0.4 mile, then turn right into the park. Enter the park and drive 0.2 mile to a four-way intersection. The road leading left heads to the recreation center. Take the road leading right toward family shelters, open play area, nature pavilion, and restrooms. After parking, return to the four-way intersection and join the asphalt trail leading north, to your right, as you are walking toward the recreation center. GPS trailhead coordinates: N37° 37' 32.53" / W77° 35' 14.71"

The Hike

Henrico County can pack a lot into their parks, and Deep Run Park offers a good example of this. Not only are there multiple trails here but also numerous other facilities. The park offers traditional soccer fields, basketball courts, picnic shelters, and a very large recreation center used for meetings and such. The park also has a natural side, including a nature pavilion and boardwalk that leads to Deep Run, and ponds. This hike takes a path that heads to the quieter north part of the refuge before making a little mini-loop and then backtracking. When you come here, however, you will see joggers, cyclists, and others creating their own fitness programs that include not only these trails but also the Exercise Trail, trails that circle the park pond, and the greater network overlaying every nook and cranny of the park. So use this suggested walk as your introduction to Deep Run Park, then create your own hike!

From the trailhead leave a busy nest of trails and make your way north through prototype hickory-oak woods, heavy with white oaks and pignut hickories, complemented by holly, cedar, and sweetgum. Interpretive signage helps you identify the trees. Pignut hickories grow throughout the Old Dominion. Virginia colonists used them extensively for tool handles, wagon wheels, and even in textile looms. Its name derives from its being a favorite food of hogs, which ranged freely back in those times. The tree was also known as "broom hickory" because it was often cut and made into broom handles. Pignut hickories range from Florida west to the Ozarks, north to Michigan, and east to the Atlantic Coast as far north as Connecticut. At Deep

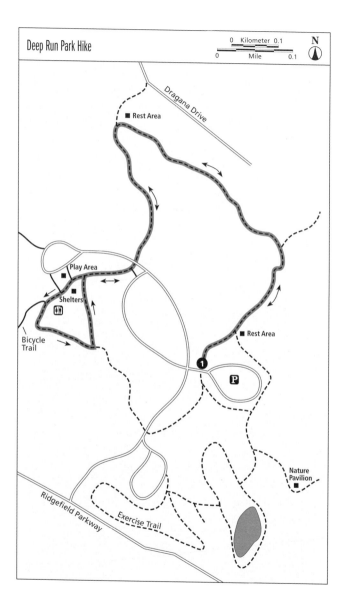

Deep Run Park Hike

Dragana Drive

■ Rest Area

■ Rest Area

Play Area

Shelters

Bicycle Trail

1

P

Nature Pavilion ■

Ridgefield Parkway

Exercise Trail

0   Kilometer   0.1

0   Mile   0.1

N

Run, the hickory nuts are consumed by squirrels, which populate the park in large numbers.

The path is shaded nearly throughout the entire hike, making it a good summertime destination. Occasional user-created paths spur off the main trail. After returning to the primary park road, the hike makes its mini-loop, passing another set of park facilities. After doing this hike once, the other trails of the park will draw you in for exploration. Have fun creating your own loop.

Miles and Directions

0.0 Start hiking north on an asphalt path, away from the four-way road junction. Shortly, pass a rest area with benches and intersect a path coming up from the parking area that also connects to the nest of trails south of here.

0.3 A spur trail leads right toward a gated fence. Stay left. Pines increase the forest diversity.

0.5 Reach a trail junction and rest area. Here a trail leads right to a neighborhood while this hike makes a hard left, now descending.

0.7 Cross the main park road and reach a junction. Stay right here.

0.8 Reach the loop portion of the hike. Keep forward here, traveling past picnic shelters, a play area, parking, and restrooms.

0.9 The Bicycle Trail leads right and loops around the soccer fields. Stay left.

1.0 Reach another trail junction. Here a path heads forward over a short bridge then leaves right toward the Exercise Trail parking lot after passing behind the recreation center. Stay left.

1.1 Complete the loop portion of the hike. Begin backtracking.

1.9 Return to the trailhead and parking area where you started, completing the hike.

2 Three Lakes Triple Loop

Combine this short trek with a visit to the elaborate nature center here at Three Lakes Park. The nature center, which overlooks the middle lake of the three impoundments, focuses on the plants and animals of the area and includes a freshwater aquarium. After your tour, do the triple loop, circling around each of the three watery destinations on easy level paths. Anglers should bring a pole.

Distance: 1.3-mile triple loop
Approximate hiking time: 1 to 1.5 hours
Difficulty: Easy
Trail surface: A little asphalt, mostly gravel and natural surfaces
Best season: Year-round
Other trail users: Anglers, bicyclists
Canine compatibility: Leashed dogs permitted

Fees and permits: No fees or permits required
Schedule: Dawn to dusk year-round
Maps: Three Lakes Park and Nature Center; USGS map: Richmond
Trail contacts: Three Lakes Park and Nature Center, 400 Sausiluta Dr., Henrico 23227; (804) 262-5055; www.co.henrico.va.us/rec

Finding the trailhead: From exit 41A on I-295 northeast of downtown Richmond, take US 301/VA 2 south (Chamberlayne Avenue) for 1.7 miles to Wilkinson Road. Turn left onto Wilkinson Road and follow it for 0.9 mile, then turn right onto Sausiluta Drive. Follow Sausiluta Drive, which will shortly dead-end into the park nature center. GPS trailhead coordinates: N37° 37' 6.27" / W77° 25' 48.95"

The Hike

Talk about turning a lemon into lemonade! The lakes of the park and around which this hike travels were borrow pits. The fill from these pits was used on site work for I-95 back in the 1950s. So what was once literally "the pits" is now a scenic destination where we can hike and learn more about the nature of central Virginia.

I can only wish the park were bigger and the trails a little longer. However, if the hike seems a little short for you, make the circuit a second time. Two of the three lakes allow fishing. Lake 2—beside the nature center—is off limits to anglers. You can enjoy this lake from the back deck of the nature center, which extends over the water. This is the shallowest lake and is good habitat for amphibians. Also, watch for bird life in these lakes. The nature center offers replicas of thirty-six birds that inhabit these parts and live amphibians and reptiles in glass tanks.

Your triple loop travels clockwise, circling the biggest water-filled pit, Lake 1, first. This lake has a picnic shelter and popular fishing pier. A stream feeds freshwater into it, then flows out. Note the two small islands within it. A mix of trees shades the path—pine, river birch, cedar, sweetgum, and tall oaks. The gravel track is mostly level, and it sometimes travels along a berm at the lake's edges.

Note the bubbling machines in the lakes, pumping oxygen into the water, which makes it more suitable for aquatic life. Lake 2 is shallow. Lake 3 has a land peninsula popular with anglers. Try to incorporate your hike with a visit to the nature center. Its hours vary, so call ahead for exact times.

Three Lakes Triple Loop

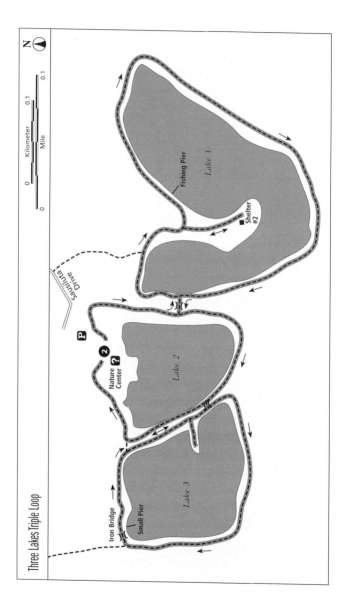

Miles and Directions

0.0 As you face the nature center, look left for a sign stating TRAIL. Lake 2 and the nature center will be to your right when you begin hiking on a wide gravel track to shortly reach a bridge. Head left, crossing the bridge over a wooded ravine to reach Lake 1.

0.2 A paved path comes in from the left. Stay right, joining the paved path as it heads toward Shelter #2. Just ahead, stay left again, as a trail extends to the peninsula and shelter on Lake 1. Shortly reach the fishing pier on your right, where the pavement ends and the gravel track resumes.

0.3 Bridge a creek entering the lake from your left. Continue curving around Lake 1.

0.4 Look for old concrete piers away from the lake, likely part of the borrow pit excavation equipment.

0.5 Bridge the creek as it leaves Lake 1.

0.7 Cross the bridge connecting Lake 1 and Lake 2, and turn left to begin circling Lake 2.

0.8 Cross a bridge and reach Lake 3. Turn left and begin circling it on a narrow irregular berm. Note the swampy woods on the far side of the berm.

1.0 Reach an iron bridge. A trail keeps forward but stay along the lake, crossing the bridge over a ravine.

1.1 Turn right at a junction as a path leads left to the nature center. Head out to the peninsula on Lake 3. This is a popular fishing spot.

1.2 Take the bridge to Lake 2. Return to the nature center on a narrow, rooty berm.

1.3 Arrive back at the nature center.

3 Pony Pasture Rapids Loop

Enjoy shoals and beaches along the James River at this popular water lover's destination. The hike then takes you amid wetlands and to a wildlife blind and also along a small stream named Pleasant Creek. The rich forest features some notably large trees.

Distance: 2.2-mile loop
Approximate hiking time: 1.2 to 1.8 hours
Difficulty: Easy
Trail surface: Natural surfaces
Best season: Year-round, though high summer may be steamy
Other trail users: Bicyclists, runners
Canine compatibility: Leashed dogs permitted

Fees and permits: No fees or permits required
Schedule: Open sunrise to sunset
Maps: Exploring the James Guide; USGS map: Richmond
Trail contacts: James River Park, 4001 Riverside Dr., Richmond 23225; (804) 646-8911; www .jamesriverpark.org

Finding the trailhead: From the intersection of Powhite Parkway and Forest Hill Avenue southwest of downtown Richmond, take Forest Hill Avenue west for 0.8 mile, then turn right onto Hathaway Road. Follow Hathaway Road for 0.3 mile as it turns into Longview Drive. Stay forward here as Longview Drive meets Rockfalls Drive after 0.7 mile. Turn right onto Rockfalls Drive then immediately bear left on Riverside Drive. Go just a short distance on Riverside Drive then turn right into the Pony Pasture parking area. The trail starts in the northeast corner of the parking lot, near the James River. GPS trailhead coordinates: N37° 33' 3.7" / W77° 31' 12.4"

The Hike

Pony Pasture Rapids is yet another tract of James River Park. The locale has not only hiking trails but also paddler accesses, natural beaches, and sunning rocks that attract swimmers and water lovers of all types. Nice days, especially in spring and early summer, will quickly fill the parking lot with those wanting to get in the water. The trails attract hikers, runners, and nature lovers as well.

The trail system takes you along the James River past a beach and along the intriguing shoreline before meeting the peninsula of land between Pleasant Creek and a wetland back from the river. More trails wander through the wetlands before returning to the trailhead.

Start on a wide trail leading from the parking area. Visitors looking to lounge in the sun or play in the water are usually upstream of the trails. At normal water levels the Pony Pasture Rapids are Class II and are often used by beginner paddlers to "break into" Richmond's 7-mile stretch of white water. Spur paths lead to the water's edge. Half Moon Beach offers a clear view of the James. Here, the water laps against tan sands. Pet owners will often be playing with their dogs in the river here. Return to thick woods of sycamore, tulip trees, sassafras, hackberry, and walnut with ample brush where thick vines aren't already draping. Watch for some very large trees in the forest, especially sycamore. The trail is easy as it wanders easterly through a wide flat. The roar of the Pony Pasture Rapids fade and is replaced by birdsong.

The eastern half of the hike travels through wetlands. Here, you can sneak up to a pond and observe wildlife through a viewing blind. This area is much less visited than

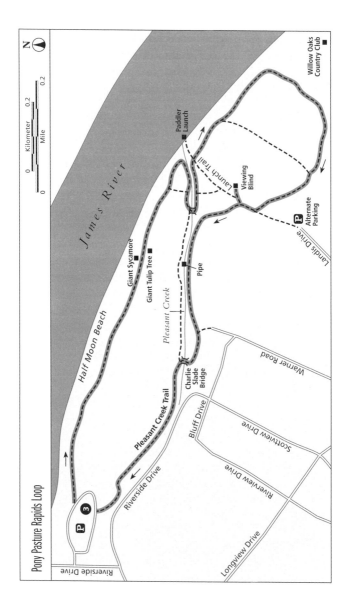

Pony Pasture Rapids Loop

James River

Half Moon Beach

Giant Sycamore

Giant Tulip Tree

Pleasant Creek

Pipe

Pleasant Creek Trail

Charlie Slade Bridge

Paddler Launch

Launch Trail

Viewing Blind

Alternate Parking

Landis Drive

Willow Oaks Country Club

Warner Road

Scottview Drive

Bluff Drive

Riverview Drive

Riverside Drive

Longview Drive

Riverside Drive

P 3

N

Kilometer
0   0.2

Mile
0   0.2

the parklands near the rapids. Your westerly return journey takes you along Pleasant Creek to the trailhead.

Miles and Directions

0.0 Look for the marker indicating the R. B. Young Riverside Trail in the northeast corner of the parking area. Join the wide shady path among user-created trails.

0.2 Reach Half Moon Beach, where you'll have a good view of the James River, Williams Island upstream, and the lower Pony Pasture Rapids.

0.5 Pass a noticeably large sycamore on trail left. A large tulip tree stands on trail right just beyond this.

0.6 Reach an intersection; a trail leads right to bypass the peninsular tip between James River and Pleasant Creek. Keep forward to reach this point of land. Curve away from the James, now along Pleasant Creek, reaching the other end of the bypass.

0.8 Cross a bridge leading left over Pleasant Creek as the Pleasant Creek Trail keeps forward. Beyond the bridge, stay left, now heading downstream along Pleasant Creek, passing a spur trail leading right to the Launch Trail leading from Landis Drive to the paddler launch on the James.

0.9 Reach a four-way intersection with the Launch Trail. The Launch Trail leading left heads to a paddler launch on the James. Shortly reach another intersection where a path heads away from the river, making an inner loop in the wetlands area. Keep forward to reach the eastern park boundary, separated from Willow Oaks Country Club by a small ditch, then curve south away from the James. Note the contrast between the woods through which you walk and the manicured landscape of the country club.

1.2 Intersect the inner loop, then pass over a small hill.

1.4 Intersect the other end of the wide Launch Trail. Turn right here, aiming for the James.

1.5 The loop hike leads left but first go straight forward on the Launch Trail just a short distance and then head right toward the pond viewing blind. Here, slips in a wooden wall allow you to observe birds in a still pond. Backtrack, then begin heading toward the trailhead, coming alongside Pleasant Creek in piney woods.

1.7 Cross a small wooden bridge then pass a pipe crossing Pleasant Creek. Don't use it as a bridge.

1.8 A user-created trail leads left to a dead end on Warner Road. Keep going straight and join a land berm heading west.

1.9 Cross Pleasant Creek on the Charlie Slade Bridge then stay left at the intersection, keeping west for the trailhead on the Pleasant Creek Trail.

2.2 Arrive back at the parking area.

4 Rockwood Park Loop

Rockwood Park, a green oasis in Chesterfield County's South Side, is the setting for this loop, just one of the many trails in this multipurpose park. Gregory's Pond is a scenic highlight of the hike. It also bridges intermittent streams and uses boardwalks to span other wetlands.

Distance: 1.7-mile loop

Approximate hiking time: 1 to 1.5 hours

Difficulty: Easy, although there are some hills

Trail surface: Asphalt, pea gravel, natural surfaces

Best season: March through May, September through November

Other trail users: Runners, bicyclists

Canine compatibility: Leashed dogs permitted

Fees and permits: No fees or permits required

Schedule: 7:30 a.m. to dusk

Maps: Rockwood Park Trail System Map; USGS map: Chesterfield

Trail contacts: Rockwood Park, 3401 Courthouse Rd., Richmond 23236; (804) 276-6661, www .chesterfield.gov

Finding the trailhead: From the intersection of Chippenham Parkway (VA 288) and Hull Street/US 360, southwest of downtown Richmond, take Hull Street/US 360 east for 4.4 miles. Turn left onto Courthouse Road and follow it for 0.1 mile to the main park entrance. Follow the signs to the nature center, which you'll reach after 0.4 mile. The hike starts in the southeast corner of the parking area, away from the nature center. GPS trailhead coordinates: N37° 27' 2.67" / W77° 34' 48.98"

The Hike

Rockwood Park, coming in at 163 acres, is the oldest of the Chesterfield County parks. It has undergone many incarnations over time and now is split between developed recreation such as baseball and basketball courts but is still mostly natural woods, where an extensive trail network runs through rolling terrain. This particular loop follows the longest natural surface loop in the park, the Orange Trail. All the park trails add up to over 4 miles of path.

The natural area is bordered on its north and east ends by Falling Creek. Gregory's Pond is formed by the damming of Falling Creek, making the eastern border a scenic locale where park meets pond. Be apprised the pond is privately owned and no fishing is allowed from Rockwood Park. The park nature center has wildlife displays and even a few critters in there.

The asphalt White Trail is your entry into the path network. White oaks dominate the woodland here, with smaller populations of sweetgum and holly, along with ample hickories and pines. Shortly come along Gregory's Pond. The forty-one-acre impoundment is bordered by the park on one side and private homes on the other. Short spur trails lead to observation points.

Gregory's Pond narrows as you circle around a watery cove to make another trail junction. Trail intersections are many, but the trails are color-coded, marked, and signed so well that even the most directionally challenged hiker would have a hard time getting lost. Occasional intermittent streambeds are crossed by bridges and boardwalks. Along the way you'll pass an interesting spot—an old ice pit. In the days before electricity area residents would cut ice blocks from the pond in winter then carry them to the pit, layering it in moss and pine boughs, then use the ice well into the summer for refrigeration. Watch for a huge white oak on your left just beyond the ice pit.

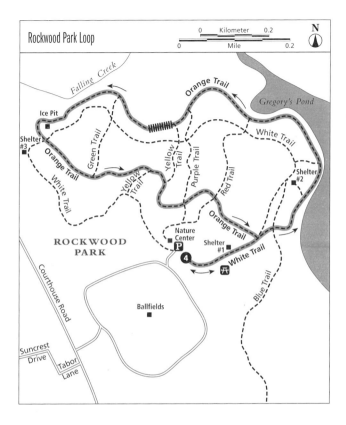

The Orange Trail wanders through the outer edges of the park, traveling from the east edge all the way to the west edge before running out of land and curving back to complete its loop. After a few trips to Rockwood, you may want to experiment and make up your own hike.

Miles and Directions

0.0 Pick up the White Trail leading from the end of the parking area farthest from the nature center. A sign states to shelters #1 and #2. The asphalt track tunnels into woodland, passing a picnic area on your right then Shelter #1 on your left.

0.1 Intersect the Orange Trail. Here, the White Trail keeps forward as an asphalt track while the Orange Trail leads right over a pea gravel and natural surface. Pick up the Orange Trail, shortly passing the Blue Trail. Begin curving along Gregory's Pond.

0.3 A spur trail leads left uphill toward Shelter #2. The Orange Trail keeps straight, undulating along the shoreline of Gregory's Pond, passing a spur trail leading to the White Trail.

0.5 Intersect the Red Trail. It leaves left 0.3 mile to the nature center. The Orange Trail keeps straight along Gregory's Pond for a short distance before turning into full-blown woodland along a streambed.

0.7 Meet the paved Purple Trail. It leads left 0.3 mile to the nature center. The Orange Trail keeps straight and shortly meets the Yellow Trail, then crosses a wetland boardwalk. The Yellow Trail leads left and shortcuts the Orange Trail.

0.8 Meet the Green Trail. It leads left to short-circuit the loop. Falling Creek is visible in the distance to your right.

1.0 Pass the old ice pit then intersect the paved White Trail. Keep straight to intersect the Green Trail a second time.

1.3 Keep going east and intersect the Yellow Trail, running in conjunction with it for a short distance, then meet the Purple Trail and Red Trail a second time.

1.6 Complete the loop portion of the hike when you meet the White Trail yet again. Turn right here and backtrack.

1.7 Arrive back at the nature center parking lot.

5 North Bank Trail

This hike travels the North Bank Trail along the James River. Here, you can view river rapids and head to a popular sunning and swimming spot—if the river is low enough. Even if the water is up, hike this track through lush woods and beside massive boulders before reaching an outflow of the Kanawha Canal.

Distance: 2.0 miles out and back

Approximate hiking time: 1 to 1.5 hours

Difficulty: Easy, but has a hill and some rock hopping

Trail surface: Natural surfaces

Best season: Year-round, though high summer may be hot

Other trail users: Bicyclists, joggers, sunbathers, anglers

Canine compatibility: Leashed dogs permitted

Fees and permits: No fees or permits required

Schedule: Open sunrise to sunset

Maps: Exploring the James Guide; USGS map: Richmond

Trail contacts: James River Park, 4001 Riverside Dr., Richmond 23225; (804) 646-8911; www.jamesriverpark.org

Finding the trailhead: From exit 74A on I-95 in Richmond, take the Downtown Expressway to the Meadow Street exit. Head south on Meadow Street, and travel 1.1 miles to Kansas Avenue. Turn left onto Kansas Avenue and follow it for 0.2 mile to Texas Avenue. Turn right onto Texas Avenue, which dead-ends at the parking lot for the North Bank Trail. GPS trailhead coordinates: N37° 31' 50.61" / W77° 28' 7.03"

The Hike

The North Bank Trail is a strand of the greater James River Park trail network. So named because it travels the north bank of the James through downtown Richmond, the path runs from the Robert E. Lee Bridge near Belle Isle to the Boulevard Bridge. It is often used by mountain bikers, but the segment where this hike takes place leads to a popular swimming and sunning place known as Texas Beach. Texas Beach got its name from the Texas Avenue access, from which this hike begins. Exploring this area is dependent on water levels in the James River, as a trail runs along the main shore but connects to other paths running along islands that border the mainland. At low water, it is simply a matter of trekking across dry channels to the islands. At other times, rock hopping can be done between the islands. And when the river is high, prudent hikers will stick to the mainland.

If you make it to Texas Beach, that's fine, but the main shore itself offers a lush forested walking path that accesses smaller beaches and avails good views of the river. At high water, you are forced to backtrack after a mile if going upstream due to an outflow of the Kanawha Canal. Hikers are trespassing if they use the adjacent CSXT Railroad bridge to cross the outflow, plus it isn't exactly safe. So use common sense and, after making the trailhead, make your own adventure.

The trail can be busy on nice, warm weekends. Expect to see joggers, anglers, sunbathers, swimmers, and others. The trail's beginning can be confusing as multiple user-created paths form a spider web. But they come together and all lead either downstream toward the Robert E. Lee Bridge or downhill to the elevated pedestrian bridge crossing the Kanawha Canal and CSXT Railroad to reach the north bank of the James. Heading upstream, it isn't long before a series of islands rises between you and the main river. It is on these islands and on rocks where sunbathers will repose. The channels between the islands seem narrow compared to the hundreds-of-feet-wide James. Rocky rapids and swift water will fill the channels when the James is up. These same channels will trickle at low water and make island hopping more doable.

Smart hikers will find out the flow rate of the James before endeavoring on a hike here. Go to the United States Geological Survey real-time water data Web site. The gauge is "James River near Richmond, VA" and the site is www .waterdata.usgs.gov/nwis/uv?02037500. If the river gauge is at 5 feet or higher, do not island hop. If it is lower, consider island hopping. Adventurous hikers on a low-water day can make it all the way to Moreland Bridge—without trespassing.

Miles and Directions

0.0 Take the dirt trail from the east end of the linear Texas Avenue access to North Bank Park. Immediately enter thick woods on a bluff well above the James River. Shortly descend off the bluff.

0.1 Join a bridge spanning the Kanawha Canal and the CSXT Railroad. Descend a circular tower of steps and join a trail heading upstream along the James in lush woodland. Islands separate the north bank from the main river.

0.3 Come directly alongside the James at a tiny beach. Views open across the water of the river rapids.

0.6 Come along a big flat rock that leads to more rocks. Potential rock hopping to a close island is doable even at higher water. An island trail leads to a beach overlooking a channel of the James. Backtrack to the mainland or head out to Texas Beach, which is farther out into the James.

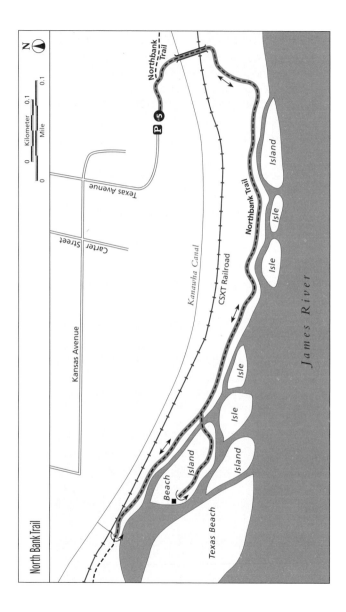

North Bank Trail

N

0 Kilometer 0.1
0 Mile 0.1

Kansas Avenue

Carter Street

Texas Avenue

P 5

Northbank Trail

Kanawha Canal

CSXT Railroad

Northbank Trail

Beach

Island

Island

Isle

Isle

Texas Beach

Isle

Isle

Island

James River

0.9 Pass over a small concrete spillway. Keep upstream.

1.0 Reach a major outflow of the Kanawha Canal, which plunges into a pool. At higher water, hikers should turn around here, though some continue the North Bank Trail by illegally using the CSXT Railroad bridge to span the outflow channel. At low flow, this is an easy crossing. Otherwise, you should backtrack.

2.0 Arrive back at the trailhead.

6 Buttermilk Loop

This hike makes a slender circuit near Reedy Creek at James River Park. It first follows the narrow and winding Buttermilk Trail, then wanders along the James, where islands await exploration. It then leaves the river and passes its namesake, historic Buttermilk Spring, before returning to the trailhead.

Distance: 2.9-mile loop
Approximate hiking time: 1.5 to 2 hours
Difficulty: Moderate
Trail surface: Natural surfaces, gravel, boardwalk
Best season: March through May, September through November
Other trail users: Mountain bikers
Canine compatibility: Leashed

dogs permitted
Fees and permits: No fees or permits required
Schedule: Open sunrise to sunset
Maps: Exploring the James Guide, USGS map: Richmond
Trail contacts: James River Park, 4001 Riverside Dr., Richmond 23225; (804) 646-8911; www .jamesriverpark.org

Finding the trailhead: From Main and Belvidere in downtown Richmond, take Belvidere/US 1/US 301 south across the James River on the Lee Bridge. Veer right onto the ramp leading to Riverside Drive. Follow Riverside Drive for 1 mile to reach the Reedy Creek entrance to James River Park. Parking is in the gravel lot after you descend from Riverside Drive. GPS trailhead coordinates: N37° 31' 25.1" / W77° 28' 13.9"

The Hike

This hike, located in the Reedy Creek area of James River Park, travels one of its premier paths—the Buttermilk

Trail—for approximately half its route. The Buttermilk Trail navigates a hilly wooded corridor under a rich forest of tulip trees, oaks, and insane amounts of ivy and other exotic ground cover, along with ferns and paw-paw. The path will occasionally divide but come together again, nestled between Riverside Drive and Norfolk Southern Railroad. Reach a tower of steps to cross the railroad then join another path wandering along the shore of the big James River. Explore 42nd Street Island, as it is connected by a bridge to the mainland. Beyond, you can walk a gravel track or take the narrow dirt paths that skirt the shore and islands along the water. Your access to other islands farther in the James depends on water levels, as many hikers rock hop or wade when the river is at 5 feet or lower, preferably much lower for this type of water walking. To find out the flow rate of the James before endeavoring on a hike, go to the United States Geological Survey water data Web site. The name of the gauge is "James River near Richmond, VA" and the site is www.waterdata.usgs.gov/nwis/uv?02037500. If the river gauge is at 5 feet or above, do not island hop. If it is lower, consider island hopping.

Fear not, for the James River has been cleaned up, as city fathers and residents alike realized the value of this aquatic resource to citizens and visitors. Before you explore islands, make sure the speed of the water matches your swimming abilities. Unfortunately, the river yearly claims foolish visitors and those who simply slip and bust their head on a rock. Be careful, James River Park needs you. If you want to become a friend of James River Park, visit www .jamesriverpark.org.

The loop continues downriver, passing the James River Park headquarters and a river access used by paddlers. This

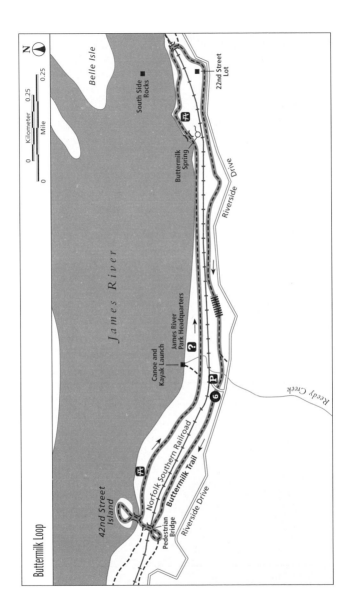

Buttermilk Loop

stretch of rapids marks where the Piedmont meets the Tidewater. The harder rock of the Piedmont remains while the Tidewater was worn away, creating this 7-mile stretch of white water that attracts boaters from central Virginia and beyond.

Come near the trailhead, but the hike has more tread to travel under large walnuts, sweetgums, and sycamores. Use a bridge to join one more island before returning to the mainland, and climb a tower that gets you over the Norfolk Southern Railroad that splits the circuit. The home stretch rejoins the Buttermilk Trail, where it passes some big trees that are overlooked. The Buttermilk Trail is popular with mountain bikers, so watch out for them. The path is designed to be used by all, so don't let this discourage you.

Miles and Directions

0.0 From the parking area, head back toward Riverside Drive and meet the Buttermilk Trail. Head right, westbound, on a single-track path in junglesque forest.

0.3 A steep section located near a metal fence has steps for hikers and a studded ramp for mountain bikers. Watch for unnatural rock piles from railroad construction days.

0.4 Pass under the pedestrian bridge crossing the railroad amid paw-paw and big beech trees. Watch for a short trail leading acutely left to reach the pedestrian bridge, as the Buttermilk Trail continues forward. Cross the railroad and descend on circular steps. Head downstream, east, on a wider trail, keeping the James River to your left. Watch for a bridge accessing 42nd Street Island and make a loop around it. User-created trails lace the isle.

0.8 Pass a picnic shelter, then come to a display explaining storm runoff and the James River. Other dirt trails run closer to the river.

1.1 Pass near the Reedy Creek parking area on your right and the canoe/kayak access trail. Look for the partly finished Powhatan dugout canoe. Bridge Reedy Creek.

1.2 James River Park headquarters stands on your left. Travel through a mix of forest and meadow.

1.6 The trail comes near the river. Look left for a bridge leading to an island. Rejoin the mainland on a small dam, which leads to Belle Isle. Consider rock scrambling on the South Side Rocks. Continue downstream.

1.8 Reach and use the pedestrian bridge crossing the railroad tracks. Enjoy views of Belle Isle from the bridge. Descend and rejoin the single-track Buttermilk Trail, now heading west, upstream.

2.0 Pass the 22nd Street parking lot. It is open only on weekends. Keep west on the Buttermilk Trail.

2.2 Meet rocked-in Buttermilk Spring, where yesteryear farmers stored their dairy before taking it to the downtown markets. Keep wandering west, passing some large tulip and oak trees.

2.6 Traverse a wetland via a boardwalk.

2.8 Reach Reedy Creek. At low flows, you can rock hop to the trailhead. At higher flows, walk to Riverside Drive then use the road bridge to reach the parking area.

2.9 Arrive back at the trailhead, completing the loop.

7 Belle Isle Loop

An Indian village, a Civil War prison camp, an iron foundry, a rock quarry, and now a city park in the middle of the James River . . . Belle Isle has been through many incarnations. Today you can enjoy hiking trails that lead to and through the island, exploring its natural beauty amid the rapids of the James as well as the historical points listed above. Interior paths extend beyond the described loop, allowing for extended rambling.

Distance: 2.4-mile loop with spurs

Approximate hiking time: 1.5 to 2 hours

Difficulty: Moderate due to hills, bridges, and diverse trail surface

Trail surface: Concrete, gravel, dirt, pavement

Best season: Year-round, though high summer may be steamy

Other trail users: Bicyclists

Canine compatibility: Leashed dogs permitted

Fees and permits: No fees or permits required

Schedule: Open sunrise to sunset

Maps: Exploring the James Guide, USGS map: Richmond

Trail contacts: James River Park, 4001 Riverside Dr., Richmond 23225; (804) 646-8911; www .jamesriverpark.org

Finding the trailhead: From exit 74A on I-95 in Richmond, take the Downtown Expressway to the first exit, Canal Street. Follow Canal Street to South Fifth Street. Turn left onto South Fifth Street and follow it to its end at Tredegar Street. Turn right onto Tredegar Street. The trail starts just before you pass under the Lee Bridge. Parking for the Belle Isle hiking trail is located near the Lee Bridge on the north side of Tredegar Street. Hourly parking is also available at the Civil

War Visitor Center on Tredegar Street. (Both lots are open after 9:30 a.m. weekdays to deter commuter parking.) GPS trailhead coordinates: N37° 32' 3.9" / W77° 26' 53.7"

The Hike

This hike is one of the most interesting anywhere for multiple reasons. Part of James River Park, Richmond's fantastic set of destinations astride the James River, Belle Isle is first reached on an innovative and exciting pedestrian suspension bridge hanging *under* the Robert E. Lee Bridge, US 1/301. It then descends to Belle Isle, where a trip exploring layers of Virginia history unfolds.

A forest overlays granite on this sixty-five-acre teardrop-shaped island. Reach a flat once you're on the isle—the place where Powhatans farmed and Yankee soldiers were later kept, and where horses were raced. The loop trail heads upstream along the James, passing Hollywood Rapids, named for the cemetery across the river. These Class III–IV rapids eat boats yearly. Head to the rocks where white water flows and herons feed. Belle Isle sits amid the 7 miles of shoals that played a major role in Richmond's founding and very placement on the map.

Ahead, the trail curves past a quarry where granite was extracted. The main pit is now a fishing pond. Reach a picnic shelter and the west island tip. Civil War gun emplacements stand atop the hill, and a trail leads right to First Break Rapid.

More history waits ahead as you curve around the island's south side. Here lies a millrace and remains of an old plant used to power the electric trolley system on the north bank downtown. A spur trail leads to the "South Side Rocks," a series of massive boulders great for hopping, normally with little water between them. This access trail travels over the head of the millrace that funneled water into the hydro plant. An iron forge from an earlier time greets hikers as they meet the south side access to Belle Isle.

Your adventure isn't over when you return to Lee Bridge. A trip to the island's east tip offers extensive river and downtown views, as well as the preserved remains of the Old Dominion Iron and Steel Company, which operated here. Yet more trails meander among the hills of the island center if you wish to explore further. Be apprised the interior trails can be confusing, as mountain bikers have created additional paths other than the official ones.

Miles and Directions

0.0 Join the paved path westbound along Tredegar Street and arrive under the Robert E. Lee Bridge. Turn up the path, looping to the suspension bridge under the Robert E. Lee Bridge. Cross the James River, enjoying stellar views.

0.4 Return to land and reach Belle Isle. From here, head right, upstream along the James River, passing near the old Civil War prison site, and reach the loop portion of the hike. Stay right, entering woodland of sycamore, as another path heads uphill to the island interior.

0.7 Pass Hollywood Rapids. Spur trails lead to the rocks, great for sunning or accessing the water. An old quarry site lies ahead.

0.8 On your left, pass the still Quarry Pond with a fishing dock. This loop keeps west along the margin between the still pond and raucous river rapids.

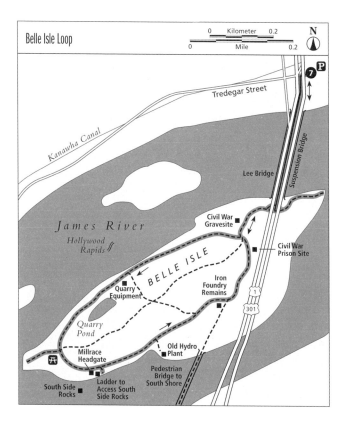

Belle Isle Loop

Kilometer 0 — 0.2
Mile 0 — 0.2

N

Tredegar Street

Kanawha Canal

Lee Bridge

Suspension Bridge

James River

Hollywood Rapids

Civil War Gravesite

Civil War Prison Site

BELLE ISLE

Quarry Equipment

Iron Foundry Remains

Quarry Pond

Millrace Headgate

Old Hydro Plant

Pedestrian Bridge to South Shore

South Side Rocks

Ladder to Access South Side Rocks

1 301

0.9 Reach a picnic shelter and a spur trail leading right to the island head. Another trail leads left and uphill to gun emplacements. After checking out the island head and First Break Rapid, curve around to the quiet south side of island.

1.1 A spur trail leads right across the millrace headgate to a ladder accessing the South Side Rocks.

1.3 Pass the old hydro plant on your right. It is not a safe place to explore.

1.4 Reach a trail junction. Here, a wide track leads acutely left to the island's interior.

1.5 Pass the brick wall of an iron foundry then reach an intersection. Here, a trail leads right to the James's south shore. This loop heads left back in the flats near the Robert E. Lee Bridge.

1.6 Complete the loop portion of the hike, then head right, heading toward the east island tip, passing under the Old Dominion Iron and Steel Company frame.

1.8 Reach the east end of Belle Isle. Great views of the city and the James River. Begin backtracking to the trailhead.

2.4 Arrive back at the trailhead.

8 Floodwall/Slave Trail

Enjoy downtown panoramas and shoals of the James River as you trace an elevated floodwall. Next join the Slave Trail through woods along the river. End at historic Manchester Docks before retracing your steps. Bring your camera—the views of Richmond and the river are unparalleled from the floodwall.

Distance: 4.4 miles out and back

Approximate hiking time: 2 to 2.5 hours

Difficulty: Moderate, some hiking in the sun

Trail surface: Asphalt, gravel, concrete, mulch, natural surfaces

Best season: September through May

Other trail users: Exercising office workers

Canine compatibility: Leashed dogs permitted

Fees and permits: Park entrance fee required

Schedule: 7:30 a.m. to dusk

Maps: Exploring the James Guide, USGS map: Richmond

Trail contacts: James River Park, 4001 Riverside Dr., Richmond 23225; (804) 646-8911; www .jamesriverpark.org

Finding the trailhead: From Main and Belvidere in downtown Richmond, take Belvidere/US 1/US 301 south across the James River on the Lee Bridge. Turn left onto Semmes Avenue (US 60) just after crossing the James River. Follow Semmes for 0.5 mile to a signed lot on the left of the road, just before the intersection of Semmes and Seventh Street. The trail leaves from the back of the parking area, away from Semmes Avenue. GPS trailhead coordinates: N37° 31' 38.9" / W77° 26' 41.2"

The Hike

This hike offers stellar vistas as well as glimpses into Richmond's past. Though the floodwall wasn't built with recreation in mind, it has become an integral link in the James River Park trail system. The top of the floodwall acts as an elevated pathway from which you can view the lowermost rapids of Richmond and downtown beyond as well as panoramas of the city's south side. Beyond the floodwall the hike joins a wooded corridor bordering the James River. Here, you can enjoy an urban woodland walk and end up at Ancarrow's Landing, also known as the Manchester Docks. At this point turn around and enjoy both paths once more. Like other downtown trails, these routes have been ingeniously integrated into existing infrastructure. The engineering feats to include these trails show foresight and determination, and Richmonders are lucky to have this hike so near downtown.

Floods have plagued Richmond throughout its history. The worst floods in recent years have come on the heels of hurricanes. The floodwalls, which are on both sides of the James, were begun in 1988 after two decades of planning. Only the south-side wall has a walkway atop it. From the trailhead parking area, it takes a little wrangling to make the floodwall, but join it shortly after passing under the Manchester Bridge. The views then come nonstop as you look out on the iconic skyscrapers of Virginia's capital city and the unruly rapids of the James. Expect to see herons, geese, and other watery wildlife in the river below, and wood debris piled up against the rocks. The old Manchester Canal, now just a quiet waterway on the backside of the floodwall, once took boats around the river rapids.

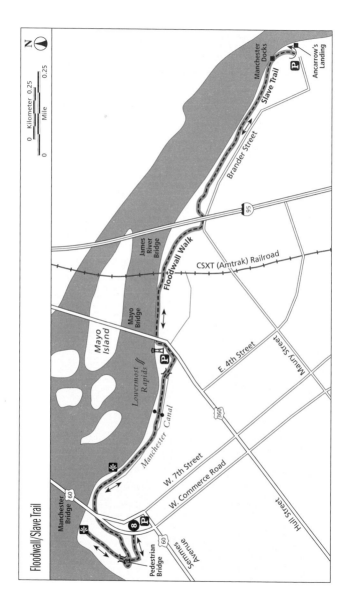

Floodwall/Slave Trail

The Floodwall Walk works past Mayo Bridge, then you travel inside the floodwall. Note the graceful arches of the Mayo Bridge. The first Mayo Bridge, made of wood, was erected in 1784. The concrete one you see replaced that one. Briefly join a levee then descend to Maury Street, where it passes under I-95 and then joins the Slave Trail. The scenery changes from a sun-splashed elevated walk to a riverside riparian forest jaunt in a matter of feet. The sounds of I-95 fade. Revel in the lush forest. As you merge onto the Manchester Docks, the weighty stone walls beside the James were actually installed in the late 1800s to handle heavy cargo. The docks were made of wood back in the days when slaves were first unloaded here in the late 1700s and later shipped to the Deep South to work newer plantations in the 1800s. The grassy area at the dock site is now a popular fishing venue. The trail then leaves the grassy area and wanders a short bit through the woods to emerge onto the parking area and boat ramp accessible by Brander Street.

Miles and Directions

0.0   With your back to Semmes Avenue, follow the concrete walkway leading toward the James River. Pass under the Manchester Bridge and travel west to shortly reach a pedestrian bridge crossing the Norfolk Southern Railroad.

0.1   After crossing the pedestrian bridge, you can head right following an old railroad grade to an elevated vista of downtown. The Manchester climbing wall is just below. However, to reach the floodwall, head left after the bridge and descend to reach a trail junction. Pass under the Manchester Bridge a second time, now heading east, downstream along the James River.

0.4   Join the floodwall, officially named the Floodwall Walk.

0.6 Reach a designated vista point, which offers a postcard view of the heart of Richmond. Old Manchester Canal is to your right.

0.8 Cross over a gate in the floodwall through which a railroad track passes, then drop off the floodwall.

0.9 Bridge the Manchester Canal.

1.0 Reach Hull Street. Turn left here, passing an alternate trail parking area, then come to circular steps leading to an elevated vista. Keep on Hull Street toward the Mayo Bridge, passing through a floodwall gate, then veer left, descending, and pass under the Mayo Bridge, resuming an easterly direction. A spur trail leads left to the lowermost rapids of the James.

1.4 Pass under the CSXT rail bridge.

1.5 Reach Maury Street, turn left, pass through the floodwall and under I-95, then join the Slave Trail, short for Manchester Slave Docks Trail.

2.1 Open onto a grassy area at the Manchester Docks. Keep along the waterfront.

2.2 Reach the trail's end after passing through a short strip of woodland and making the Ancarrow's Landing parking lot. Backtrack to Semmes Avenue.

4.4 Arrive back at the Semmes Avenue parking lot near Seventh Street.

○9 Canal Walk

This urban hike travels through Richmond's downtown along restored canals dug to circumvent rapids of the James River. Now, downtown looms over the canal, a watery window to Richmond's past. The Canal Walk is hard surface its entire distance as it works through the modern infrastructure while reliving history through informational displays.

Distance: 2.0-mile figure-eight loop
Approximate hiking time: 1.5 to 2.5 hours
Difficulty: Easy
Trail surface: Concrete
Best season: Year-round
Other trail users: Commuters, history buffs, runners, diners
Canine compatibility: Leashed dogs permitted

Fees and permits: No fee or permit required
Schedule: Mostly 24/7/365 except for Brown's Island
Maps: Canal Walk; USGS map: Richmond
Trail contacts: City of Richmond, 900 East Broad St., Richmond 23219; (804) 646-7000; www .richmond.gov

Finding the trailhead: From exit 74A on I-95 in Richmond, take the Downtown Expressway to the first exit, Canal Street. Follow Canal Street to South Fifth Street. Turn left onto South Fifth Street and follow it to its end at Tredegar Street. The trail starts near the intersection of Tredegar and Fifth Street at the bridge onto Brown's Island. Parking here is tricky at best. Hourly parking is available at the Civil War Visitor Center on Tredegar Street, or you can park at the Belle Isle hiking trail locale under the railroad tracks beyond the museum. (Both lots open after 9:30 a.m. weekdays.) GPS trailhead coordinates: N37° 32' 5.61" / W77° 26' 41.10"

The Hike

The City of Richmond has poured a lot of money into downtown revitalization generally and the Canal Walk specifically. It seems to be working. Now, visitors can travel along the restored canals of downtown, learn about history through displays, and enjoy the watery views as well as food, fun, and entertainment, plus get a little exercise while doing it. So, don't feel bad when you order extra cream in your latte while watching others travel the multimillion-dollar route ingeniously laid out through and under—even over—the downtown infrastructure.

The route is marked and signed, not only for directions but also with historical information. It is a must-see for history buffs. Strategically located call phones are there to ease your downtown walking worries. It'll be hard to get up a head of steam as you stop and learn some of the information on the medallions laid into the gravel-embedded concrete walkway, as well as other signage. Water borders the route nearly its entire way, which adds scenic value to the historic overlay.

The route is amazingly linked together. First the walkway bridges Brown's Island and explores that piece of land before saddling alongside the Haxall Canal, passing piers of the rail bridge that brought Jefferson Davis to his inauguration as president of the Confederate States of America. See where the world's first electric trolley traveled. Of course the canals themselves are historic, built in the late 1700s through the 1800s to allow boats to travel around the rapids of Richmond, expanding commerce. When the first part of the first canal was opened in 1790, it was the first commercial canal in the United States. Remember, these canals were hand dug. Visit the cross laid by early English explorer Christopher Newport, who interacted with the Powhatan Indians stationed along the rapids of the James River. The Triple Crossing is the world's first three-way railroad inter-section.

While here, you may want to take a boat cruise on the lower Tidewater Connection Locks. Tickets can be had at the New Turning Basin.

On your return trip, look beyond the walk at the high rises of downtown and the river in the distance, thinking about how the canals of Richmond were begun in 1784, surveyed by none other than George Washington himself.

Miles and Directions

0.0 With your back to the Civil War Visitor Center at Tredegar, leave Tredegar Street to join Brown's Island on a dam/bridge. Once on Brown's Island, pass the Powhatan Chief-dom and Manchester & Free Bridges informational medal-lions inlaid into the path. Continue east along Haxall Canal. View rapids of the James.

0.2 Pass under the Manchester Bridge. An arched iron pedes-trian bridge leaves left across the canal. This will be your return route.

0.5 Pass within the roofless walls of an old hydroelectric plant.

0.6 Reach the end of the Haxall Canal near the Christopher Newport Cross. Turn left toward Twelfth Street, passing the Reynolds plant, then join the Tidewater Connection Locks, using steps. Shortly cross over to the north side of the lock then pass under the Thirteenth Street Bridge, then cross back over to the south side of the canal.

0.8 Pass under the Virginia Street Bridge. Emerge at the New Turning Basin, where boat tours are available.

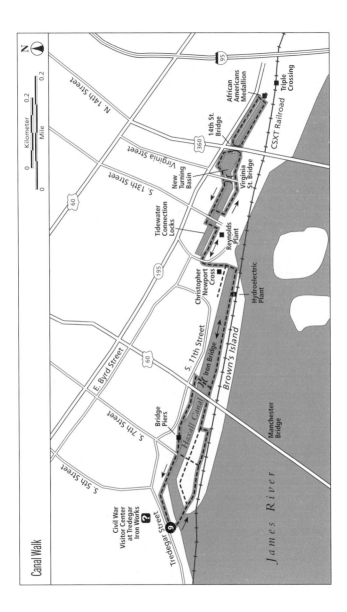

Canal Walk

James River

N

Kilometer 0.2
Mile 0.2

Tredegar Street

Civil War Visitor Center at Tredegar Iron Works

S. 5th Street

S. 7th Street

Bridge Piers

E. Byrd Street

195

60

S. 11th Street

Christopher Newport Cross

Haxall Canal

Iron Bridge

Brown's Island

Hydroelectric Plant

Manchester Bridge

Tidewater Connection Locks

Reynolds Plant

New Turning Basin

Virginia St. Bridge

Virginia Street

S. 13th Street

N. 14th Street

14th St. Bridge

African Americans Medallion

CSXT Railroad

Triple Crossing

95

60

360

1.0 Reach the Triple Crossing. Head back to the north side of the canal near the African Americans information medallion and the Waterfront informational medallion. Turn back up the canal here, though the trail extends to Dock Street under I-95 and is slated for more expansion.

1.2 Curve around the north side of the New Turning Basin and the tour boat ticket area. Continue under the Thirteenth Street Bridge and the Tidewater Connection Locks to reach the Reynolds plant again. Backtrack up the south side of the Haxall Canal.

1.7 Reach the arched pedestrian bridge to cross the Haxall Canal and walk new terrain. Pass under the Manchester Bridge. Climb steps near the Seventh Street roundabout auto access. A larger pedestrian bridge connects Seventh Street to Brown's Island. Head west along an elevated path, paralleling Tredegar Street.

2.0 Arrive back at the trailhead.

10 Dorey Park Loop

This walk travels along a park lake then joins gravel trails through woods and finally a path named the "Exercise Trail" to make a loop that is worth a visit. The park as a whole is well kept and maintained, so consider incorporating a picnic or even a little fishing into your adventure.

Distance: 1.9-mile loop
Approximate hiking time: 1 to 1.5 hours
Difficulty: Easy
Trail surface: Asphalt, gravel, natural surfaces
Best season: March through May, September through November
Other trail users: None
Canine compatibility: Leashed dogs permitted

Fees and permits: No fees or permits required
Schedule: 7:30 a.m. to dusk
Maps: Dorey Park; USGS map: Dutch Gap
Trail contacts: Dorey Park, 1031 7200 Dorey Park Rd., Henrico 23231; (804) 795-2334; www .co.henrico.va.us/rec

Finding the trailhead: From exit 22 on I-295 southeast of downtown Richmond, take VA 5 west (New Market Road) for 0.6 mile to Doran Road. Turn right onto Doran Road to meet Darbytown Road. Turn left onto Darbytown Road and follow it for 1.5 miles to reach Dorey Park on your left. Enter the park, passing the recreation center, and drive to the back of the park near Picnic Shelter #2 and Dorey Lake. GPS trailhead coordinates: N37° 27' 37.5" / W77° 20' 25.5"

The Hike

This 400-acre park is located on the site of the Dorey Farm. The facilities have expanded and changed over the park's history, since it was established in 1984. Most visitors come to play or watch the soccer, softball, or baseball on the many fields here. You can play tennis or disc golf, even fish. Despite all the other attractions, many a walker and hiker find their way onto the paths here, especially locals on daily exercise regimens.

The hike first curves around five-acre Dorey Lake. The lake was part of a program to put urban anglers and fishing destinations together. The fishery is managed by the Virginia Department of Game and Inland Fisheries. You will likely see shore anglers setting up near the trailhead. You will also see ample bird life in the translucent lake. The hike shortly leaves the water to enter hickory-oak woodland on a gravel track. Pines, maple, and sassafras diversify the flat woods. The trail meanders north, keeping a tributary of Four Mile Creek to your left. It then curves southbound and joins a little nest of trails, one of which is the Exercise Trail, though it is hard to identify which path is "the" Exercise Trail.

Pass picnic shelters amid Virginia pines. This evergreen, named after the Old Dominion, is identified among many others here at the park with interpretive signage. It is a pioneer tree, meaning it will grow in old fields and on disturbed areas in poor soils, where other trees can't grow. This area was probably a field before the park was established and the Dorey Farm was in full swing. The park then allowed the forest to regrow here, and Virginia pines were one of the first to regenerate. The pines provide shade for other tree species to grow, then they die off in a process known as succession. Virginia pines are used primarily for pulpwood. Though named for this state, these pines range from New York down to Mississippi.

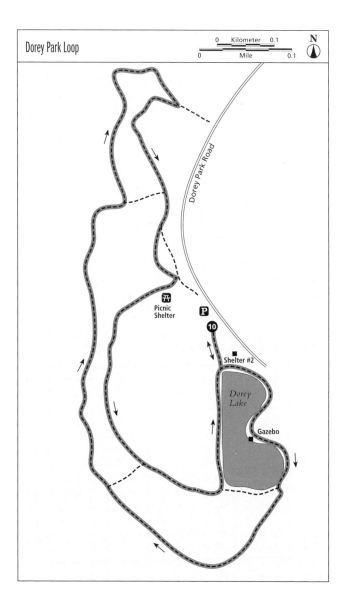

Dorey Park Loop

0   Kilometer   0.1
0   Mile   0.1

N

Dorey Park Road

Picnic Shelter

P

10

Shelter #2

Dorey Lake

Gazebo

The nest of trails near the hike's end may prove confusing, but you certainly won't get lost. The correct route will lead back to the pond, where you can make one last watery walk before returning to the trailhead.

Miles and Directions

0.0 As you face Dorey Lake near Picnic Shelter #2, join an asphalt track, walk just a few feet, then veer left around Picnic Shelter #2 and curve around the northeast side of the water. Shortly pass a pier and gazebo, while looking over the lake fountain.

0.2 Leave Dorey Lake after passing over the lake outflow. Enter full-blown woodland on a wide gravel track.

0.3 Pass through a gas line clearing.

0.5 Pass a shortcut trail leading right.

0.6 Pass through the gas line clearing a second time.

0.9 A spur trail leads right to shortcut toward picnic shelters across a small field.

1.0 The loop turns sharply east.

1.1 Reach a trail junction. A spur path leads to the main park road. Now head southbound, entering a nest of trails, one of which is the Exercise Trail.

1.3 Come to a parking area. Turn right here, passing behind shelters #4–#7. Continue curving around the back of the developed facilities.

1.6 Reach an intersection. Here, one of the shortcut trails leads right. Keep straight toward Dorey Lake.

1.7 Dorey Lake comes into view. Turn left here, cruising up the west side of the lake on a paved trail. The gazebo stands across the water.

1.9 Arrive back at the trailhead.

11 Dutch Gap Loop

This preserved wildland near the famous re-created Henricus Village of the 1600s offers a big loop hike where you can become one with the wetlands along the James River in lower Chesterfield County, and visit the village.

Distance: 4.7-mile lollipop loop
Approximate hiking time: 2.2 to 3 hours
Difficulty: Moderate, but only because of distance
Trail surface: Natural surfaces, gravel
Best season: September through May
Other trail users: Bicyclists
Canine compatibility: Leashed dogs permitted

Fees and permits: No fees or permits required
Schedule: Hours vary by season; call ahead or check Web site
Maps: Henricus Historical Park and the Dutch Gap Conservation Area; USGS map: Hopewell, Chester
Trail contacts: Chesterfield County Parks & Recreation, P.O. Box 40, Chesterfield, VA 23832; (804) 706-9690; www.co.chester field.va.us or www.henricus.org

Finding the trailhead: From exit 61A on I-95 south of downtown Richmond, take VA 10 east toward Hopewell for 0.4 mile to reach a light. Turn left onto Old Stage Road (SR 732). Travel for 2 miles then turn right onto Coxendale Road (SR 615). Follow Coxendale for 0.7 mile then turn right onto Henricus Park Road. Continue for 1.2 miles to reach the park. The hike starts in the rear of the Henricus Visitor Center. GPS trailhead coordinates: N37° 22' 27.3" / W77° 21' 43.2"

The Hike

In its current incarnation, Dutch Gap is a conservation area of over 800 acres, covering lands and waters of the old James

River channel where wildlife thrives. Long ago, English colonists settled in the area, forming Henricus, a community around which a defensive ditch was built. The moat became known as the Dutch Gap. Fast forward: As commercial traffic increased on the James River, a canal was cut across a loop in the James, forming a big oxbow lake. Later, the interior of the oxbow was mined for sand and gravel. The company dug a channel to haul the product to ports on the James, turning the landscape—er, waterscape—into what we see today. Now Dutch Gap is preserved and you can make a loop around these wetlands on one of the better treks in the greater capital area. Add a tour of old Henricus, where life ways of the 1600s are displayed in a re-created village, and you have one fine day in the Old Dominion!

The trail itself follows a double-track path through woods and along water, with plenty of spur trails to extend your hike. A mix of sun and shade accompanies the trail, though most areas are more shaded than not. Bring a hat if you are sensitive to Sol. Views are plentiful as the hike is often along water. In winter, leafless trees enhance viewing prospects. Spur trails and docks offer open looks, too.

Despite being in an industrial area, Dutch Gap exudes a surprisingly wild atmosphere. Interestingly, even though the mouth of the James is 80 miles distant, the waters here are tidally affected, though entirely fresh. By the way, boaters like to enjoy the old river channel and the interior lagoon via a paddling trail, so you could incorporate a paddling trip into your adventure as well.

Miles and Directions

0.0 From the parking area, walk toward the visitor center and join a wide gravel track heading behind the left side of the

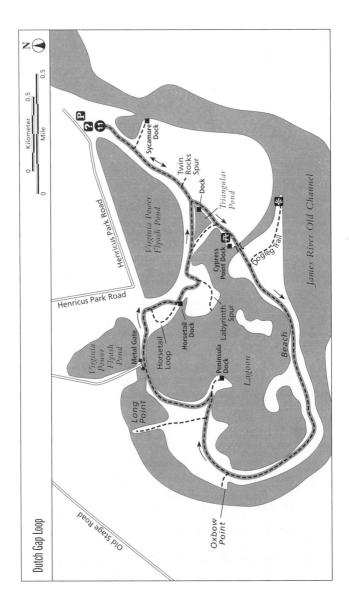

Dutch Gap Loop

building as you face it. The elevated and fenced Virginia Power flyash pond rises to your right.

0.2   A spur trail leads left to Sycamore Dock. Keep forward.

0.5   A spur trail leads left to the Twin Rocks.

0.6   Begin the loop portion of the hike. Stay left here, passing a triangular pond on your right with a dock. Just ahead a spur trail leads right, connecting your return route. Keep forward, still heading southwest.

0.9   Reach the channel connecting the inner lagoon to the old James River. Cypress Point Dock and a picnic shelter stand to your right. Cross the channel on an arch iron bridge. Just ahead the Dogleg Trail heads to the old James River channel. Continue wandering the measure of land between the lagoon on your right and the old James River channel on your left.

1.8   Begin curving northwest, mimicking the old river channel.

2.3   A spur trail leads left to Oxbow Point. The main path continues curving with the old oxbow.

2.6   A spur trail leads left to a man-made peninsula, Long Point, extending into the old river channel.

2.7   Reach a trail junction. Here a spur trail leaves right to Peninsula Dock. Stay left, now on a more substantial gravel road, temporarily leaving the conservation area on Virginia Power property.

3.1   Meet a gate. A road leaves left, but stay right, leaving the gravel track and traveling along a second flyash pond.

3.4   Reach the Horsetail Loop. It leads right through grass, which can be overgrown in summer.

3.5   Reach the other end of the Horsetail Loop and the Horsetail Dock.

3.7   The Labyrinth Spur leads right to old sunken barges that now act as islands.

3.8   Come back along a flyash pond and turn right.

3.9 Return to the triangular pond and a trail heading southeast. Keep straight toward the visitor center.

4.1 Complete the loop portion of the hike and begin backtracking.

4.7 Arrive back at the visitor center.

12 Dodd Park Loop

This hike takes you through attractive woods down to Ashton Creek Marsh, where a long boardwalk offers a firsthand look at this wetland. The hike then saddles alongside the Appomattox River, where more views await. Be apprised this hike does have some hills as it descends and ascends along a river bluff.

Distance: 1.6-mile loop
Approximate hiking time: 1 to 1.5 hours
Difficulty: Moderate due to hills
Trail surface: Gravel and natural surfaces
Best season: March through May, September through November
Other trail users: None
Canine compatibility: Leashed dogs permitted

Fees and permits: No fees or permits required
Schedule: 7:30 a.m. to dusk
Maps: R. Garland Dodd Park at Point of Rocks; USGS map: Hopewell
Trail contacts: R. Garland Dodd Park at Point of Rocks, 201 Enon Church Rd., Chester 23831; (804) 706-9690; www.chester field.gov

Finding the trailhead: From exit 61A on I-95 south of downtown Richmond, take VA 10 east for 3.1 miles to Bermuda Orchard Lane. Turn right onto Bermuda Orchard Lane and dead-end into Enon Church Road (SR 746) after 1.6 miles. Turn right onto Enon Church Road then make a quick left into R. Garland Dodd Park at Point of Rocks. Enter the park and keep forward, passing ballfields and tennis courts, seeking the old Homestead area on your right. There is a little rustic cabin here. The trail starts in the back of the field to your right as you face the cabin. GPS trailhead coordinates: N37° 19' 18.21" / W77° 21' 17.45"

The Hike

This is a hike you wish were longer amid a trail system that you wish was in somewhat better repair. Maybe it will be when you get here. Though it has seen better days, the trails are certainly in well enough shape to use and are walked by many visitors. The natural setting is a bluff overlooking the confluence of Ashton Creek and the Appomattox River. Your hike first drops off the bluff then cruises a boardwalk with a great wetland view. And if that weren't enough, it comes to another area where the trail overlooks the Appomattox River and Cobb Island standing across from it. The downside is a minor maze of user-created paths that aren't on the park map. It would be almost impossible to get lost here, however, as the 188-acre park is bordered by Ashton Creek on the west, the Appomattox River on the south, and the developed side of the park and Enon Church Road on the north and east. So fear not, but be ready to perhaps do a little doubling back as you learn the trail system.

The hike first leaves the old Homestead area then descends along a moist hollow rich with mountain laurel before reaching the bottoms along Ashton Creek. A lush forest of holly, oak, hickory, beech, and buckeye flank the trail. The slope is impressive. Reach the Marsh Overlook, where you can look out toward the Appomattox River across the Ashton Creek Marsh. What a view! Then comes the nearly 0.5-mile walk on the boardwalk that travels over the marsh and offers a unique chance to be one with the wetland. Take your time here, watching for wildlife and also gaining up-close views of the watery locale.

The hike then joins the Appomattox River. Look for hints of past land use: a graded road, old fence wire, and dug pits. This is also the location of the Appomattox Overlook, where you can gain a sweeping view of the river and of Cobbs Island beyond. An elevated platform enhances the panorama. A mix of field and forest accompanies you while traveling alongside the Appomattox. Finally, ascend the bluff and complete the hike.

Miles and Directions

0.0 As you face the Homestead, look in the right-hand corner of a field for a trail sign. Begin following the wide path downhill, descending wooden steps.

0.1 Reach a four-way trail junction. Here, a spur path leads left back up to the Homestead and your return route keeps forward. Turn right here and descend to cross a bridge over a streambed. Once across the bridge turn right and uphill, creating the longest loop possible.

0.4 Reach the Marsh Overlook. Here you can look down upon the Ashton Creek Marsh. Descend by steps as a shortcut trail comes in on your left. Join the boardwalk across Ashton Creek Marsh. The boardwalk is actually a floating aluminum structure connected every few feet by joints. Traverse the heart of the lily pads and open waters that comprise the wetland.

0.6 Bridge open water over a tidal stream.

0.8 Reach the end of the boardwalk. A shortcut path leads left back toward the Homestead area. Pass the now-closed Causeway Trail. Stay right here, curving around to reach the Appomattox River and an overlook. Stay along the trail closest to the water, curving northeast along the Appomattox.

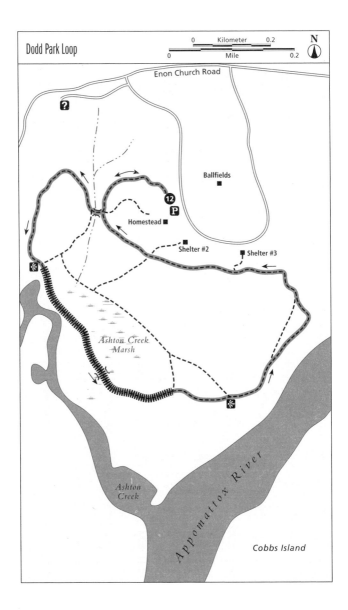

Dodd Park Loop

0   Kilometer   0.2

0   Mile   0.2

N

Enon Church Road

?

Ballfields

12 P

Homestead ■

Shelter #2 ■

Shelter #3 ■

Ashton Creek
Marsh

Ashton
Creek

Appomattox River

Cobbs Island

Watch for a small beach below the trail. Other trails lead to the water.

1.1 Turn away from the Appomattox River.

1.2 A spur trail leads right up to Shelter #3. Keep walking the margin between the hillside to your right and bottomland to your left.

1.4 Reach a four-way junction. A spur trail leads right up to Shelter #2. Another leads left toward the bottoms. Keep straight.

1.5 Complete the loop portion of your hike at a trail junction. You can either keep straight and backtrack or head right uphill to emerge at the Homestead.

1.6 Arrive back at the trailhead.

13 Harrison's Creek Loop

This hike explores part of Petersburg National Battlefield. The now wooded lands offer a natural respite contrasting with the dark Civil War days. Start at a replicated siege site, then travel a well-marked trail network that passes along Harrison's Creek, which was an important battle line during the siege of Petersburg. Other parts of the loop traverse historic roads used then.

Distance: 3.4-mile loop
Approximate hiking time: 1.7 to 2.1 hours
Difficulty: Moderate, due to a few hills
Trail surface: Natural surfaces, gravel
Best season: Year-round
Other trail users: Bicyclists, equestrians
Canine compatibility: Leashed dogs permitted

Fees and permits: Park entrance fee required
Schedule: 9:00 a.m. to dusk
Maps: Petersburg National Park Eastern Front Trails, USGS map: Prince George
Trail contacts: Petersburg National Battlefield, 1539 Hickory Hill Rd., Petersburg 23803; (804) 732-3531; www.nps.gov/pete

Finding the trailhead: From exit 52 on I-95 in Petersburg, take Wythe Street (VA 36) for 2.5 miles to the battlefield. Head to the visitor center, pay your entry fee, obtain a map, then join the Park Tour Road. Follow the Park Tour Road 1 mile to tour stop #3, on your left. GPS trailhead coordinates: N37° 13' 57.5" / W77° 21' 16.0"

The Hike

Petersburg National Battlefield preserves the site where the Union laid siege to Confederates who were attempting to protect Petersburg and its important railroad supply lines. Without these supply lines reaching Richmond, the Confederate capital city would fall to the Union—so thought Union general Ulysses S. Grant, after failing to take Richmond by frontal assault. He then set about capturing Petersburg, which led to the extended blockade. This hike travels the Eastern Front section of the preserved battlefield on well-laid-out trails that travel through now pleasant woodland where men once lived and died for their respective causes.

The loop leaves a tour stop that details soldier life and siege tactics during the siege of Petersburg. It then cruises double-track paths, passing alongside Harrison's Creek. This quiet stream slips through shady woodland, giving no hint of its importance as a battle line where Union and Confederate soldiers faced one another. Beyond Harrison's Creek the trail passes a large tulip tree that was likely a witness to the siege. It then curves to the eastern edge of the battlefield, joining old Meade Station Road, an important army provision route during the siege. Finally the hike loops back on the historic Prince George Court House Road.

The trails are all in great shape, and most intersections are marked with a concrete post similar to those used at Shenandoah National Park. Each concrete post has a corresponding letter, keeping you apprised of your whereabouts. The trails themselves are blazed in red or yellow. Red-blazed trails are open to hikers and bicyclists, whereas the yellow-blazed paths are open to hikers, bicyclists, and equestrians. Interpretive trails are open to hikers only. The rolling terrain is canopied with hardwoods, cedars, and pines. Sweetgum, dogwoods, and hickories fill out the tree list. The park service manages the forest using prescribed fire, and you may see evidence of this, especially along the Battery 7 Trail. The last part of the hike travels historic roads that played a role in the siege.

Miles and Directions

0.0 With your back to the parking area near post C, take the wide trail heading south on the Attack Road Trail, not toward the standing monument.

0.2 Intersect the Water Line Trail. Keep forward.

0.3 Reach post B and a three-way intersection. Turn right here onto the Harrison's Creek Trail.

0.8 Harrison's Creek Trail turns north.

0.9 Reach post R. Here, the Birney Trail leaves left, while the Harrison's Creek Trail curves right. Shortly reach post Q. Here, the Water Line Trail leaves right. Keep straight on the Harrison's Creek Trail, now on a single-track path meandering through piney woods.

1.3 Cross Park Tour Road and reach tour stop #4. Harrison's Creek is within sight to your left. Keep along Harrison's Creek, imagining gallant Confederates and cowardly Union soldiers facing each other across the creek.

1.4 Reach post N. Here, a trail leads right to the old picnic area. Stay left and reach post M, and join the Friend Trail. Turn right, climbing away from Harrison's Creek.

1.7 Pass near a huge trailside tulip tree. Another large tulip tree stands ahead.

1.9 Cross a tributary of Harrison's Creek.

2.0 Climb to make post L and Park Tour Road. Keep straight, joining the Battery 7 Trail as it nears a cloverleaf connecting park roads to VA 36.

2.5 A red-blazed trail leads right toward post K. Keep straight, shortly passing another red-blazed trail leading right. Travel level lands.

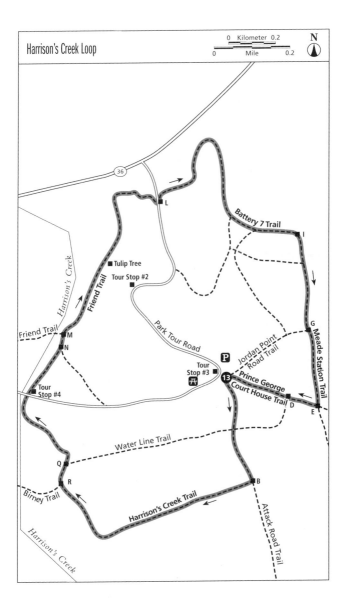

2.7 Reach post I. Turn right and head due south on Meade Station Trail. This path follows the supply line used by Union soldiers during the siege. Shortly pass a red-blazed trail leading right.

2.9 Reach post G. Here, the Jordan Point Road Trail leads right to tour stop #3. Keep forward, still on the Meade Station Trail. Bridge a stream by culvert.

3.1 Reach post E to meet Prince George Court House Trail, which was used by both armies to haul men and supplies. Turn right, joining the old road-turned-path.

3.2 Reach post D. Here, the Water Line Trail leaves left. Keep forward on the Prince George Court House Trail.

3.4 Arrive back at tour stop #3, completing the loop.

14   Encampment Loop

This hike circuits the Poor Creek drainage of Petersburg National Battlefield. Leave the site of Fort Haskell and travel through bottoms, hills, and by the old Taylor Farm, all playing roles in the Union siege of Petersburg. Along the way, look for earthworks dug by soldiers during the ten-month blockade, the longest in American history.

Distance: 2.7-mile loop
Approximate hiking time: 1.5 to 2 hours
Difficulty: Moderate, due to a few hills
Trail surface: Natural surfaces
Best season: Year-round
Other trail users: Bicyclists, equestrians
Canine compatibility: Leashed dogs permitted

Fees and permits: Park entrance fee required
Schedule: 9:00 a.m. to dusk
Maps: Petersburg National Park Eastern Front Trails; USGS map: Prince George
Trail contacts: Petersburg National Battlefield, 1539 Hickory Hill Rd., Petersburg 23803; (804) 732-3531; www.nps.gov/pete

Finding the trailhead: From exit 52 on I-95 in Petersburg, take Wythe Street (VA 36) for 2.5 miles to the battlefield. Head to the visitor center, pay your entry fee, obtain a map, then join the Park Tour Road. Follow the Park Tour Road to tour stop #6, on your right. GPS trailhead coordinates: N37° 13' 57.5" / W77° 21' 16.0"

The Hike

The ten-month siege of Petersburg was one of mostly boredom for the soldiers of the Confederacy and the Union, but it was interspersed with battles. One such encounter was the Battle of Fort Stedman on March 25, 1865. General

Lee determined to pierce Union lines, take Grant's military railroad, then concentrate his troops to fight Grant more effectively. The Rebels blasted through the Yankee lines but weren't able to hold their position and were pushed back. This hike starts at the earthworks of Fort Haskell, where tightly packed Bluecoats repulsed the Confederate charge. From this point you head south to the site of the Taylor Farm, where nothing but a brick foundation remains from its Civil War destruction. The loop then wanders amid earthworks still faintly visible under a lush forest.

The trails here at the Eastern Front of Petersburg National Battlefield are well marked and maintained, with intersections marked by concrete posts with an accompanying letter. The entire loop is open to hikers, bicyclists, and equestrians. Much of the loop is single-track path as it meanders through woods and fields, a favorable situation for deer and turkey.

The first part of the hike uses the Poor Creek Trail, a single-track path traveling southbound in classic pine-oak-hickory woods, roughly paralleling Park Tour Road on one side and Poor Creek on the other. A keen eye will spot manipulated land, whether it is from the siege or later as farms. Look for level spots, lines of trees, and even aged forest. Ironically, the path nears the Norfolk Southern Railroad. Petersburg was a rail hub during the Civil War and was the reason for Grant marking it for takeover. The hike then reaches tour stop #7, where the Taylor family plantation, Spring Garden, was left in ruins. You can now see brick foundations of a home, lying in repose atop a quiet grassy knoll, contrasting an earlier violent time. The balance of the loop joins the mostly wooded Encampment Trail, where trenches and earthworks lace the forest amid occa-

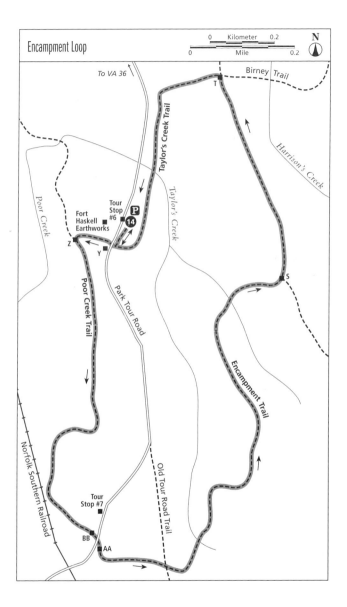

Encampment Loop

0   Kilometer   0.2

0   Mile   0.2

N

To VA 36

Birney Trail

Taylor's Creek Trail

Harrison's Creek

Taylor's Creek

Tour Stop #6

P

14

Fort Haskell Earthworks

Z

Y

Poor Creek

Poor Creek Trail

Park Tour Road

S

Encampment Trail

Norfolk Southern Railroad

Old Tour Road Trail

Tour Stop #7

BB

AA

sional streambeds. A final couple of turns on the Taylor's Creek Trail bring you back to the trailhead.

Miles and Directions

0.0 From tour stop #6, walk across the road to visit the earthworks of Fort Haskell. Then walk south down Park Tour Road to reach a trail and post Y. Head back into the woods after passing alongside the earthworks. Walk just a short distance to reach post Z and the Poor Creek Trail. Head left on the Poor Creek Trail, joining a southbound single-track path.

0.5 The Poor Creek Trail curves west, nearing fields.

0.7 The Poor Creek Trail comes within sight of the Norfolk Southern Railroad then pops out onto a field, aiming for tour stop #7.

0.8 Reach post BB and tour stop #7. Atop the hill to the north stands the brick foundation of the Taylor home. Their farm was destroyed during the war. Cross Park Tour Road, reach post AA, then begin the Encampment Trail as it heads east.

1.0 Cross Old Tour Road Trail, shortly turning north.

1.1 Bridge upper Taylor's Creek. Watch for earthworks on the forest floor.

1.7 Dip to span another tributary of Taylor's Creek.

1.8 Reach post S. Here, the Encampment Trail heads left, joining a wide old roadbed, while a spur trail leads right for a horse trailer parking area near park headquarters.

2.2 Reach post T and a four-way intersection. Turn left, westbound, now on the Taylor's Creek Trail.

2.4 Bridge Taylor's Creek. Shortly pass the parking area for tour stop #6. Keep forward, following the Taylor's Creek Trail to where it officially meets Park Tour Road.

2.7 Meet the Park Tour Road and walk back to the parking area.

15 Beaver Lake Loop

This hike explores a wetland/lake deep in the heart of Pocahontas State Park. Trailside scenery includes watery vistas from two observation piers, rolling woods, a wetland boardwalk, and the site of an old mill along Third Branch. You can also visit the Civilian Conservation Corps Museum located at the trailhead.

Distance: 2.5-mile loop
Approximate hiking time: 1.3 to 2 hours
Difficulty: Moderate due to hills
Trail surface: Pea gravel, boardwalk
Best season: March through May, September through November
Other trail users: None
Canine compatibility: Leashed dogs permitted

Fees and permits: Park entrance fee required
Schedule: 7:30 a.m. to dusk
Maps: Pocahontas State Park Trail Guide; USGS map: Chesterfield
Trail contacts: Pocahontas State Park, 1031 State Park Rd., Chesterfield 23632; (804) 796-4255; www.dcr.virginia.gov/state_parks/poc

Finding the trailhead: From exit 62 on I-95 south of downtown Richmond, take VA 288 north for 4.5 miles to Iron Bridge Road (VA 10 east/Chesterfield). Travel for 1.5 miles to Beach Road (SR 655). Turn right onto Beach Road and follow it for 4.2 miles then turn right into the state park. Continue past the entrance station and go 1.4 miles then turn left at the sign for the CCC Museum/Nature Center. Go a short distance then turn left into the parking area for the CCC Museum. The trail starts near the museum. GPS trailhead coordinates: N37° 23' 12.5" / W77° 34' 54.7"

The Hike

Pocahontas State Park is the premier state park destination in the greater Richmond area. Interestingly, the nearly 8,000-acre state park was known as Swift Creek Recreation Area when originally developed by the Civilian Conservation Corps in the 1930s. Later, the State of Virginia took over the preserve. It was renamed Pocahontas State Park on the suggestion of a student winner of a contest renaming the park. Beaver Lake, the body of water around which this hike takes you, was originally dammed by the CCC boys. After eighty years it is silting in and has become more of a wetland than lake. No problems though; Beaver Lake is great for wildlife, and the hike takes you both along the lake and through the hills surrounding it. An early morning or late evening visit may result in your seeing some of the critters that call Pocahontas home.

The trail system here at Pocahontas is well marked and maintained, and the Beaver Lake Loop is no exception. You will follow a pea gravel track most of the way. Trail intersections are clearly signed, eliminating any confusion. Attractive woodland of maple, holly, and white oak shades the path as it borders the water. Cattails and water lilies provide cover for bass and catfish. Frogs will serenade you on your trek. Then the sounds of falling water reach your ears as you curve around the lake spillway and begin your circuit walk of Beaver Lake.

Beech and tulip trees find their place in the lakeside woodland. Squirrels skitter away from your feet. The hills lead you to a bluff that offers wintertime views to an overlook of Beaver Lake. Along the way you will also encounter some history. Long before it was a park, the area was settled by small farmers. To grind their corn Third Branch was dammed for its waterpower. You will pass the site of this mill during the loop. Third Branch is a clear, tan-tinted stream that flows over sandbars. The sandbars draw kids and dogs to the small shaded creek at the crossing. The creek continues to draw as you follow it downstream toward Beaver Lake, joining wetland boardwalks where land and water meld. Here, moisture-tolerant vegetation such as sycamore and paw-paw line the path and add to the biodiversity. Enjoy more of the wetland wonderland and lake views before concluding the hike. If you desire more trail to tread, join the Ground Pine Loop near the end.

Miles and Directions

0.0 As you face the CCC Museum, join a wide trail leading right just a short distance to reach an intersection. Here, the blue-blazed Beaver Lake Trail keeps forward, while the Old Mill Bicycle Trail leads right. Begin meandering toward Beaver Lake.

0.2 Reach Beaver Lake. A wooden observation pier extends into the water. Head left, beginning the loop portion of the hike.

0.3 Intersect the Old Mill Bicycle Trail, then curve below the lake spillway on a wooden bridge to reach another junction. Here, the Old Mill Bicycle Trail leaves left while the Beaver Lake Trail leaves right and uphill.

0.5 Descend to bridge an often-dry stream.

0.8 Bridge a second stream.

0.9 A spur trail leads right to a bluff overlook with winter views.

1.4 Reach the old mill site and Third Branch. A concrete low-water bridge takes you across the stream. Another trail junction lies just uphill. Stay right with the Beaver Lake Trail, as a connector path keeps forward to meet the Old Mill Bicycle Trail.

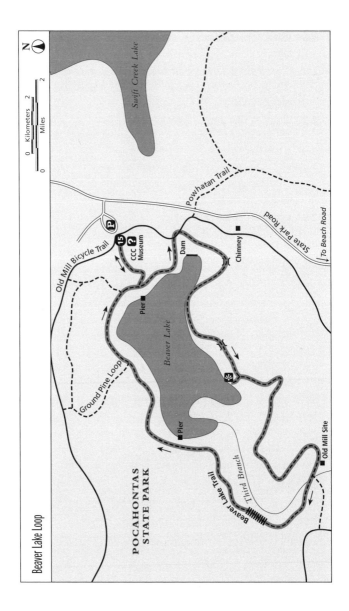

Beaver Lake Loop

POCAHONTAS
STATE PARK

Swift Creek Lake

Old Mill Bicycle Trail

Ground Pine Loop

Beaver Lake

Pier

Pier

Beaver Lake Trail

Third Branch

Old Mill Site

CCC
Museum

Dam

Chimney

Powhatan Trail

State Park Road

To Beach Road

N

0   Kilometers   2

0   Miles   2

1.6 Join a wetland boardwalk traveling the Third Branch bottoms.

1.9 Come along the shore of Beaver Lake. Here, a short pier extends into the water and offers more wildlife-viewing opportunities.

2.2 Reach an intersection. Here, the Ground Pine Loop leaves left. Join this trail if you want to extend your hike; otherwise, stay forward on the Beaver Lake Loop.

2.4 Reach the other end of the Ground Pine Loop. The Beaver Lake Trail keeps forward to shortly complete its loop. Backtrack left to the trailhead.

2.5 Arrive back at the trailhead.

16 Forest Exploration Trail

This trail loops its way on the north side of Swift Creek Lake at Pocahontas State Park. After bridging the lake, the hike travels through multiple forest ecosystems. It also explores the cultural history of the park, visiting a pioneer homesite and cemetery.

Distance: 2.2-mile loop

Approximate hiking time: 1.2 to 1.8 hours

Difficulty: Easy, but has some hills

Trail surface: Natural surfaces

Best season: March through May, September through November

Other trail users: Mountain bikers

Canine compatibility: Leashed dogs permitted

Fees and permits: Park entrance fee required

Schedule: 7:30 a.m. to dusk

Maps: Pocahontas State Park Trail Guide; USGS map: Chesterfield

Trail contacts: Pocahontas State Park, 1031 State Park Rd., Chesterfield 23632; (804) 796-4255; www.dcr.virginia.gov/state_parks/poc

Finding the trailhead: From exit 62 on I-95 south of downtown Richmond, take VA 288 north for 4.5 miles to Iron Bridge Road (VA 10 east/Chesterfield). Travel for 1.5 miles to Beach Road (SR 655). Turn right onto Beach Road and follow it for 4.2 miles then turn right into the state park. Continue past the entrance station and go 1.5 miles before turning right at the sign for the boat ramp. Follow the road past a large parking area then descend past Picnic Shelter #2 to reach the boat ramp and a footbridge over Swift Creek Lake. Start the trail by crossing the footbridge. GPS trailhead coordinates: N37° 23' 22.08" / W77° 34' 35.05"

The Hike

Pocahontas State Park is managed for both recreation and wildlife. This state park in what is now the south end of metro Richmond is easily the largest natural locale in the capital area. Having this place to hike is important, but so is preserving the natural landscape. Managing the forests to enhance wildlife is done through timber thinning, prescribed burns, and restoring natural plant species. At one time all fires were suppressed at the state park and resulted in a change of growth from its natural state, but now the park realizes that fires are a natural component of the forest, and the prescribed burns are having a positive effect. On this hike you visit various forest types and can see firsthand how forest management past and present will affect this valuable state park in the future.

The immediate trailhead lake area offers paddleboat and canoe rentals for exploring Swift Creek Lake. Bank anglers will also be found near the parking area. Attractive woodland of beech, hickory, oak, and pines with ample mountain laurel greets you on the loop. Interpretive information and resting benches are placed throughout the trek. Sweetgum, holly, and red bud fill the understory.

Park personnel use forest roads that run like veins through the park to manage the forest. Parts of the Forest Exploration Trail either follow or cross these forest roads. However, the loop is well marked and maintained, allowing you to focus on the natural beauty of the area. The beginning of the hike travels forest roads and nears Swift Creek Lake in bottomland where maple, sycamore, and paw-paw grow, more examples of forest type. Back on a ridgeline you will pass the pioneer homesite and cemetery of a

Forest Exploration Trail

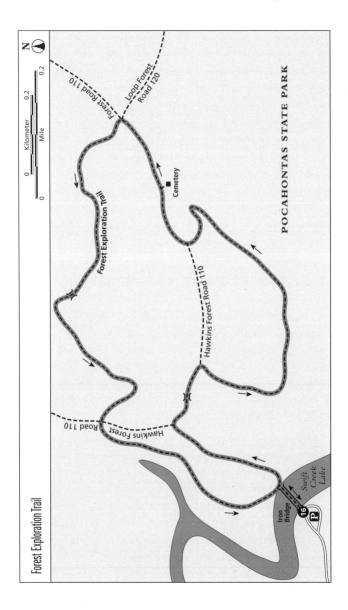

POCAHONTAS STATE PARK

N

Kilometer
0   0.2
0   0.2
Mile

Loop Forest Road 120

Forest Road 110

Forest Exploration Trail

Cemetery

Hawkins Forest Road 110

Hawkins Forest Road 110

Iron Bridge

16
P

Swift Creek Lake

nineteenth-century couple and their child. This is but one of the eighteen cemeteries identified within the boundaries of the nearly 8,000-acre state park. Look for privet and other homesteader-planted exotic species.

Other past forest practices lie ahead as you pass through a loblolly pine grove planted in 1985. Count the years from now and gauge the tree's age. Maple, sweetgum, and vines grow amid the row-cropped evergreens. The evergreen world soon falls behind as you enter a hollow full of hardwoods. Note not only the change of forest type but also smells of the woodland. In the hardwoods, look for a rocky wet weather cascade to your right. Another surprise lies downstream—some massive boulders come seemingly out of nowhere.

The final part of the hike begins aiming for Swift Creek Lake. Here, it passes through a beech forest that has evolved precisely from the lack of fire. It should be primarily oak woodland, but fire suppression has allowed the beeches to grow. You begin to see an embayment of Swift Creek Lake before coming alongside some mountain laurel, which will be showing off its pinkish white blossoms in mid-May.

Miles and Directions

0.0 Leave the parking area to join an iron span bridging Swift Creek Lake. Immediately reach a trail junction. Stay right, heading away from the lake, beginning the loop portion of your hike.

0.2 Reach a trail junction. Here, the Forest Exploration Trail turns right, joining Hawkins Forest Road 110. Dip to bridge a tributary.

0.4 Reach another junction. FR 110 keeps forward, while the Forest Exploration Trail turns right and enters bottomland.

0.9 After turning away from the bottomland, the trail ascends along a hollow and meets FR 110 again, now on a ridgeline. Here, turn right and join FR 110 a second time, traveling through partially timbered land, now regrowing in sumac.

1.0 Pass a spur trail leading right a short distance to a pioneer cemetery and homesite.

1.2 Reach a four-way trail junction. Here Loop Forest Road 120 leads right while the Hawkins Forest Road 110 keeps forward. The Forest Exploration Trail leads left and enters a loblolly pine grove.

1.5 Span a bridge over a small, clear creek just after passing some massive boulders on trail right. Travel downstream as the stream widens into a wetland.

1.8 Meet Hawkins Forest Road 110 for the last time. Keep forward, crossing the road to come alongside an embayment of Swift Creek Lake in beech woodland.

2.2 Complete the loop portion of the hike, returning to the iron bridge. Cross to the south side of Swift Creek Lake, and arrive back at the trailhead.

17 Old Mill Bicycle Trail

If you are looking for a beautiful destination and an extended hike, take the Old Mill Bicycle Trail, which wanders through Pocahontas State Park while circling Third Branch and Beaver Lake. The well-marked loop has plenty of hills, which add to the challenge.

Distance: 6.1-mile lollipop loop
Approximate hiking time: 2.8 to 4.2 hours
Difficulty: More challenging due to distance and hills
Trail surface: Gravel, natural surfaces
Best season: March through May, September through November
Other trail users: Mountain bikers
Canine compatibility: Leashed dogs permitted

Fees and permits: Park entrance fee required
Schedule: 7:30 a.m. to dusk
Maps: Pocahontas State Park Trail Guide; USGS map: Chesterfield
Trail contacts: Pocahontas State Park, 1031 State Park Rd., Chesterfield 23632; (804) 796-4255; www.dcr.virginia.gov/state_parks/poc

Finding the trailhead: From exit 62 on I-95 south of downtown Richmond, take VA 288 north for 4.5 miles to Iron Bridge Road (VA 10 east/Chesterfield). Travel for 1.5 miles to Beach Road (SR 655). Turn right onto Beach Road and follow it for 4.2 miles then turn right into the state park. Continue past the entrance station then immediately park in the lot to the right of the road. The trail starts on the far side of the road from the parking lot. GPS trailhead coordinates: N37° 22' 11.2" / W77° 34' 35.4"

The Hike

Pocahontas State Park is a large state park. The developed recreation area covers but a small portion of the destination, and the rest is managed as forestland. However, the demand for trails in the greater Richmond area has grown and the park has responded, opening many of the old forest roads for trail use and establishing the Old Mill Bicycle Trail in the developed area of the park. Hikers are welcome though the trail was created for bicycles. The balloon loop travels through thick forest then circles around Third Branch and Beaver Lake, intersecting many other developed trails in the park. The loop also goes on and off numerous forest roads. However, the route is clearly signed at every junction, and you should have no concerns following the trail. Finally, even though this is a designated bicycle trail, it is only used by casual pedalers because hard-core mountain bikers go for the tougher single-track paths nested together north of this loop. The Old Mill Bicycle Trail is primarily a double-track path.

The adventure leaves the park office as a level gravel path, roughly paralleling the main park road. The trail crosses many tributaries that cut between forested hills of hickory, oak, pine, holly, and sweetgum. Don't be surprised if you see a deer darting away during your hike. This forest is full of them. In the warm season songbirds will be cheering you on. Occasional meadows form woodland openings. Third Branch is a clear-tan stream flowing over auburn sandbars and cuts a deep valley studded with bottomland hardwoods. Pines and cedars are more prevalent on the hills. Autumn olive, a brushy, exotic species with silvery green leaves, is planted by the park to provide winter food for wildlife. Trail intersections are many near Beaver Lake. Don't miss the old homestead chimney from prepark days. After completing the loop you still have 1.2 miles of backtracking, so save some energy for that.

Miles and Directions

0.0 From the parking area near the park office, cross the main park road and join the signed Old Mill Bicycle Trail on a pea gravel track. Immediately stay right as another path leads left.

0.2 Join a gated road leaving left. It is but a short distance right to the main park road.

0.5 Reach an intersection after crossing a tributary. Turn right here, heading sharply north.

0.9 Span a tributary by culvert.

1.1 Span another tributary by culvert. Ascend a hill.

1.2 Reach the loop portion of your hike. Keep forward on double track, as the return route is to your right. Begin an extended descent.

1.5 Cross Third Branch on a wide wooden bridge. Climb away from bottoms.

1.6 A spur trail leads right, downhill, toward the old mill site and the Beaver Lake Trail.

2.2 Reach a four-way intersection. Here, the Old Mill Bicycle Trail turns right, northbound.

2.6 Descend to span a tributary on a short wooden bridge. Climb into pines.

2.7 Reach a three-way junction. Stay right, rolling through hills.

3.0 Come to another three-way junction. This one turns right, heading east on what was Old Crosstie Road.

3.4 Reach the signboard and entry into the mountain bike single-track trail complex. Stay forward, still on Old Crosstie Road.

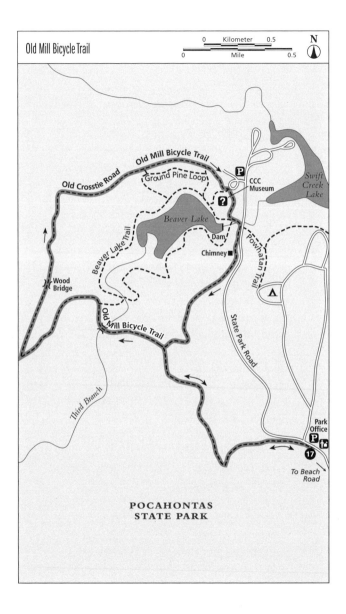

Old Mill Bicycle Trail

0   Kilometer   0.5

0   Mile   0.5

N

Old Mill Bicycle Trail

Old Crosstie Road

Ground Pine Loop

P

CCC Museum

Swift Creek Lake

?

Beaver Lake

Beaver Lake Trail

Dam

Chimney

Powhatan Trail

Wood Bridge

Old Mill Bicycle Trail

State Park Road

Third Branch

Park Office

P

17

To Beach Road

POCAHONTAS
STATE PARK

3.5 Pass the first access with the Ground Pine Loop. Keep forward on double track.

3.7 Pass the second access with Ground Pine Loop, then a parking lot to your left.

3.9 Reach the main trail parking area near the CCC Museum. The Old Mill Bicycle Trail re-enters woods on the far side of the museum, descending toward Beaver Lake Dam.

4.1 Intersect the Beaver Lake Trail. Stay left, crossing Third Branch on a low-water concrete bridge below the dam. Immediately make another intersection. Stay left here as the Beaver Lake Trail heads right toward the dam. The Old Mill Bicycle Trail ascends, passing the Powhatan Trail.

4.2 Pass a chimney from an old homesite on trail right.

4.6 Bridge a streamlet by culvert.

4.9 Complete the loop portion of the hike. Turn left and begin backtracking.

6.1 Arrive back at the trailhead.

18 **Powhite Park Loop**

This seemingly forgotten park is used mostly by nearby locals and mountain bikers. Consider making this woodsy loop, which travels the wetlands of Powhite Creek before climbing an adjacent hill then circling back to the trailhead. Be apprised that road noise from Chippenham Parkway will impact the hike. An interior nest of trails adds to the potential mileage.

Distance: 2.2-mile lollipop loop
Approximate hiking time: 1.5 to 2.5 hours
Difficulty: Moderate, due to hills
Trail surface: Natural surfaces
Best season: September through May
Other trail users: Mountain bikers
Canine compatibility: Leashed dogs permitted
Fees and permits: No fees or permits required
Schedule: 7:30 a.m. to dusk
Maps: None; USGS map: Bon Air
Trail contacts: Richmond City Parks, 4900 East Broad St., Richmond 23219; (804) 646-7000; www.ci.richmond.va.us/

Finding the trailhead: From the intersection of Powhite Parkway (VA 76) and Chippenham Parkway (VA 150) southwest of downtown Richmond, take Chippenham Parkway south 0.4 mile to Jahnke Road (SR 686). Take Jahnke east toward Richmond, immediately entering the Richmond city limits. Powhite Park is immediately on the left, but you have to go up to the first light toward Richmond and make a U-turn and then travel west on Jahnke Road to make the park entrance, across from CJW Medical Center. The trail starts at the park turnaround road. GPS trailhead coordinates: N37° 31' 5.42" / W77° 31' 39.79"

The Hike

The trails of Powhite Park are somewhat of a free-for-all, as mountain bikers continue to add paths in the park's interior. That being said, a first-time visitor can easily make a loop by staying to the outside of the many trail intersections. Only a couple of trails head away left from the loop, and they connect to adjacent neighborhoods. Furthermore, the park is surrounded by a creek on one side and residential development on the others, so if you are briefly discombobulated, just backtrack or ask a fellow hiker or mountain biker for directions. Of course, asking for directions can be troubling, especially if you are a man. This I know.

The hike has rewards. The first part travels a marshy wetland along Powhite Creek, a favorable wildlife-viewing location despite its proximity to Chippenham Parkway. The auto noise coming from the parkway actually allows you to observe waterfowl without them hearing you. The second part of the hike ascends a hill via switchbacks, which is good training if you are heading to Shenandoah National Park or some other vertically varied hiking destination. Do be on alert for mountain bikers, and extend the same courtesy as you expect from them.

The auto-accessible area of the park is very narrow, but it does have shaded picnic tables should you choose to bring lunch along. The hike begins at the circular road as a single-track path with Chippenham Parkway deafeningly close, but not for long. You walk a narrow strand of public property between the parkway and condos off to your right. Don't be discouraged—the hiking improves as the park widens.

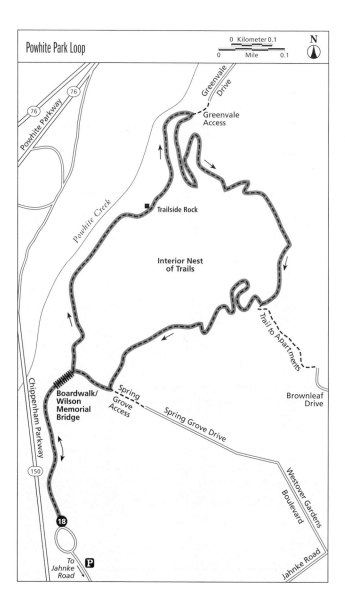

Powhite Park Loop

0 Kilometer 0.1

0 Mile 0.1

N

Powhite Parkway

76

76

Greenvale Drive

Greenvale Access

Powhite Creek

Trailside Rock

Interior Nest of Trails

Trail to Apartments

Brownleaf Drive

Chippenham Parkway

150

Boardwalk/ Wilson Memorial Bridge

Spring Grove Access

Spring Grove Drive

Westover Gardens Boulevard

18

P

To Jahnke Road

Jahnke Road

A boardwalk marks the beginning of your loop. From here begin cruising the wetlands of Powhite Creek. Cattails rise from the marsh. You may see beavers here and certainly will see evidence of their industry—chewed-down trees, tender branches stripped of their bark, perhaps even a dam or lodge. Continue threading the margin between the level wetland to your left and the rising hill to your right. A hickory-oak forest spreads up the hill. After passing a gate leading to a nearby neighborhood, the trail then begins switchbacking up the aforementioned hill. After topping the hill, the path winds back to Powhite Creek, completing the circuit.

Miles and Directions

0.0 After parking along the entry road in one of the designated spots, walk to the circular dead end and join a single-track dirt path heading north.

0.2 Reach bottomland and a boardwalk—the Wilson Memorial Bridge. Just ahead your return route leaves right. Stay left, heading clockwise on the loop.

0.6 Pass a seemingly out-of-place gray boulder to the left of the trail. Keep along the edge of wetland. Pass a second boulder.

0.8 Reach a trail junction along a fence. Here, a trail leads left through a gate to a nearby neighborhood on Greenvale Drive. The trail then turns back south and switchbacks.

1.0 Come along the park border fence line then leave it again.

1.2 Top out on a hilltop, passing a couple of old gates. The trail then meanders south on top of the plateau-like hill. Watch for a couple of old boundary gates in the forest.

1.4 A spur trail leads left to apartments off Brownleaf Drive. Keep forward, snaking west. Avoid trails heading directly down a ravine near the park boundary. Trail managers are trying to discourage use of this erosive path. Houses are visible beyond the park boundary.

1.8 Cross the ditch with the erosive trail in it.

1.9 A spur trail leads left to a neighborhood off Spring Grove Drive. Turn right, going west.

2.0 Complete the loop portion of the hike. Turn left, cross the boardwalk, and backtrack.

2.2 Arrive back at the trailhead.

19 Amelia Loop

This hike wanders a plethora of paths amid a 2,200-acre piece of land nestled against the Appomattox River in Amelia County. The trail system is composed of double-track trails that border forest and field.

Distance: 3.8-mile lollipop loop
Approximate hiking time: 1.8 to 2.5 hours
Difficulty: Moderate due to hills and potentially confusing trail junctions
Trail surface: Natural surfaces
Best season: March through May, September through November, other non-hunting periods
Other trail users: Equestrians, hunters

Canine compatibility: Leashed dogs permitted
Fees and permits: No fees or permits required
Schedule: Sunrise to sunset
Maps: Amelia Wildlife Management Area; USGS map: Chula
Trail contacts: Virginia Department of Game and Inland Fisheries, 4010 West Broad St., Richmond 23230; (804) 367-9147; www.dgif.virginia.gov/

Finding the trailhead: From the intersection of Chippenham Parkway (VA 150) and US 360 west of downtown Richmond, take US 360 west for 18 miles to Chula Road (before Amelia Court House). Turn right onto Chula Road (SR 604) and follow it for 4.8 miles to Genito Road (SR 616). Turn left onto Genito Road and follow it for 1.4 miles to Kennons Lane (SR 652). Turn right onto Kennons Lane to enter the WMA at 0.9 mile, then keep forward to a road split at 0.6 mile. The left split leads to Amelia Lake and the right split heads toward the shooting range. Stay right toward the shooting range; after 0.2 mile park at a gate, as the road going left heads to the shooting range. Do not block the gate. There will be a signboard near the road split indicating the Milking Parlor Trail. GPS trailhead coordinates: N37° 27' 55.1" / W77° 54' 50.0"

The Hike

The Appomattox River is a major tributary of the James River. Amelia Wildlife Management Area, the setting for this hike, borders the Appomattox River for approximately 3 miles. The Appomattox originates in Appomattox County and flows east for 130 miles before meeting the James near Hopewell. Interestingly, the English originally named the river Bristol, but locals ended up using the Indian name after a tribe of natives settled in the eastern part of the watershed. The Appomattox drains 1,300 square miles of central Virginia. A few streams of the Amelia WMA add to the flow, including one dammed stream forming one-hundred-acre Amelia Lake.

This hike loops along a curve of the Appomattox while traveling through an old dairy farm turned wildlife management area. The trails are interrelated double-track paths. Junctions are not signed, which can be frustrating, but hopefully won't deter you from coming here. Unfortunately, the state WMA map is not entirely accurate, which also can be frustrating. So come here early with an open mind and perhaps a GPS, then have an adventure. Be apprised the WMA does have a shooting range, open from September through March, but it is closed on Monday during that time.

The trek begins on the Milking Parlor Trail, a double-track path that follows an old farm road bordered by oaks, cedars, and pines. Make your way to the Appomattox River. The trail roughly parallels the river as it curves through fields. Take note of the crops sown for wildlife here. A dense thicket of woodland divides you from the water. Come tantalizingly close to the Appomattox to view riverside willows, but a marsh keeps you from accessing

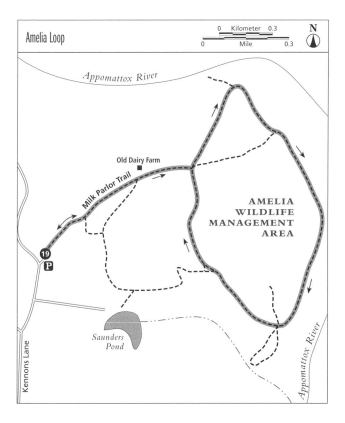

Amelia Loop

Appomattox River

Old Dairy Farm

Milk Parlor Trail

AMELIA
WILDLIFE
MANAGEMENT
AREA

19
P

Appomattox River

Saunders
Pond

Kennons Lane

the river. But this marsh is good for wildlife. After turning away from the river, the loop traverses field and forest
before returning to the old dairy farm site and backtracking
to the trailhead.

Miles and Directions

0.0 At the trailhead, pass around a pole gate. Begin following
a double-track path northeasterly. A small transmission line
runs roughly parallel to the path.

0.2 A spur trail leads right. Keep forward on the main path.

0.5 Reach the site of the old dairy farm that gave the name to the trail you are walking. A farm road leads acutely right back toward the trailhead. Keep straight, passing the dairy buildings to your left.

0.7 Reach a four-way junction in a mix of field and wood. Turn left here onto a grassy track descending toward the Appomattox River.

1.0 Make a three-way trail junction. Turn right here, now roughly paralleling the Appomattox River in a field.

1.2 Pass the east end of the Milking Parlor Trail. Shortly cut through a line of trees dividing fields. Keep straight on increasingly sloped terrain.

2.0 Reach a five-way junction. The two far left trails form a mini-loop that curves against a stream flowing out of Saunders Pond. The far right path heads up a hill. You take the trail heading west, away from the Appomattox River. This is the most used path as it enters a shady tunnel, slightly ascending.

2.7 Reach a triangular intersection where the woods give way to a large field. Stay right here, keeping the balance of the field to your left.

3.1 Complete the loop portion of your hike upon returning to a four-way junction. Turn left here, back on the Milking Parlor Trail.

3.3 Pass the old dairy farm buildings on your right. Keep forward, backtracking toward the trailhead.

3.8 Arrive back at the trailhead.

20 Powhatan Loop

This hike makes a loop on the lesser-used trails of Powhatan Wildlife Management Area. Start at one of the three angler ponds here, then wander grassy tracks through rolling woods where you may see deer, rabbit, or turkey.

Distance: 3.7-mile lollipop loop
Approximate hiking time: 1.8 to 2.5 hours
Difficulty: Moderate, due to some hills
Trail surface: Natural surfaces
Best season: March through May, September through November, other non-hunting periods
Other trail users: Equestrians, hunters
Canine compatibility: Leashed

dogs permitted
Fees and permits: No fees or permits required
Schedule: Sunrise to sunset
Maps: Powhatan WMA; USGS map: Trenholm, Powhatan
Trail contacts: Virginia Department of Game and Inland Fisheries, 4010 West Broad St., Richmond 23230; (804) 367-9147; www.dgif.virginia.gov/

Finding the trailhead: From the intersection of Chippenham Parkway (VA 150) and US 60 west of downtown Richmond, take US 60 west for 19.5 miles to Ridge Road (watch for the public fishing lake sign). Turn left onto Ridge Road and follow it 1.3 miles, then turn left onto Deer Lane, entering the WMA. At 0.5 mile, reach a loop and Bass Pond to your right; park here. The trail starts at the dam of Bass Pond. GPS trailhead coordinates: N37° 32' 36.7" / W78° 0' 27.1"

The Hike

Virginia's wildlife management areas are underutilized destinations for central Virginia hikers. Powhatan is one such place and offers Richmonders a rural retreat, a country destination to take a walk in unbridled nature, perhaps to see a deer, rabbit, or turkey, as I have. Many urban hikers are reluctant to visit places because of the hunting that takes place. Simply check the hunt dates on the Virginia Department of Game and Inland Fisheries (VDGIF) Web site, or call to find out if hunting is going on at the WMA in which you are interested, and you are good to go. The VDGIF wants visitors of all types, including hikers. That is why they developed a trail system!

The trails at Powhatan are decently marked and well maintained, and with the map in this book along with an accompanying one available as a PDF over the Internet, you should be set. Bring a picnic lunch to complement your trip or even a fishing rod to ply for bass and bream in one of the lakes here; just don't bypass Powhatan because it is a WMA.

You may see anglers in the eight-acre Bass Pond while crossing its dam. If it has been raining a lot, the trail may be sloppy near the dam outflow. Join the Squirrel Ridge Trail as it meanders through hardwoods and beside wildlife clearings. The forest here is teeming with white oaks. For wildlife the acorns are important. Deer also eat the twigs and foliage. For man, its high-grade wood is used for flooring, furniture, baskets, and interior trim. Drinkers take note: White oak is often used for the barrels in which whiskey is aged. The tree ranges throughout Virginia from the mountains to the tidewater. Its bark is a whitish color and is its primary identifying feature. White oaks range from Michigan to Florida and west to the Nebraska border then east to the Atlantic. Red bud, hickory, dogwood, sweetgum, and tulip trees round out the forest.

The hike next follows the Holly Trail, looping along the western side of Sallee Creek and stepping over a tributary.

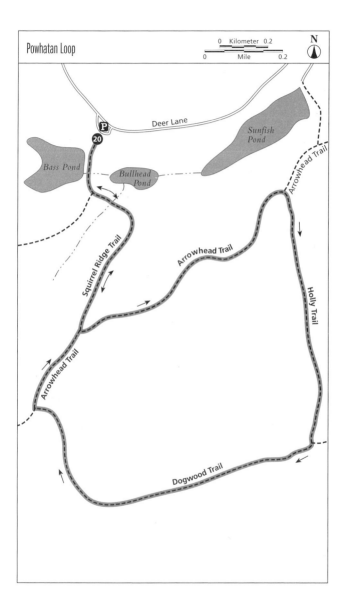

Powhatan Loop

0 Kilometer 0.2
0 Mile 0.2

N

Deer Lane

P
20

Bass Pond

Bullhead Pond

Sunfish Pond

Arrowhead Trail

Squirrel Ridge Trail

Arrowhead Trail

Holly Trail

Arrowhead Trail

Dogwood Trail

Fields border this track. The Dogwood Trail features rolling wooded hills, some open terrain, and a young low forest. The combination of different habitats adds to the birding possibilities. All too soon you are completing the loop portion of the hike and backtracking to the trailhead.

Miles and Directions

0.0 Leave the circular parking area and head south toward Bass Pond. Step around the pole gate and walk south along the earthen dam. Look left for wooden steps leading uphill into a grove of trees. Here, a grassy trail leads right toward Ridge Road. Stay left, joining the Squirrel Ridge Trail as it immediately dips to a streamlet feeding Bullhead Pond.

0.3 The Squirrel Ridge Trail levels out and passes a clearing on your left. Re-enter woods.

0.6 Reach a trail junction in a clearing. This begins the loop portion of your hike. Turn left here onto the Arrowhead Trail. The double-track path is bordered by grass, effectively creating a linear wildlife clearing.

1.3 Reach another intersection. Here, the Arrowhead Trail keeps forward. Turn right to join the grassy Holly Trail.

1.7 Descend to step over a tributary of Sallee Creek, the main watercourse traveling through Powhatan WMA. Climb surprisingly steeply to join a field.

2.0 The Holly Trail ends. Turn right here, joining the Dogwood Trail, now heading west.

2.6 Curve north and enter more open terrain.

2.9 Meet the west end of the Arrowhead Trail. A path leads left just a short distance to a gate on Ridge Road. Stay right in a grassy area.

3.1 Meet the Squirrel Ridge Trail, completing the loop portion of the hike. Backtrack toward Bass Pond and the trailhead.

3.7 Arrive back at the parking area.

About the Author

Johnny Molloy is a writer and adventurer based in Johnson City, Tennessee. His outdoor passion started on a backpacking trip in Great Smoky Mountains National Park. That first foray unleashed a love of the outdoors that has led to his spending over 120 nights in the wild per year. Friends enjoyed his adventure stories; one even suggested he write a book. He pursued his friend's idea and soon parlayed his love of the outdoors into an occupation. The results of his efforts are over thirty-six books. His writings include hiking guidebooks, camping guidebooks, paddling guidebooks, comprehensive guidebooks about a specific area, and true outdoor adventure books. Molloy has also written numerous magazine articles and for Web sites and blogs as well. He continues writing and traveling extensively throughout the United States endeavoring in a variety of outdoor pursuits. For the latest on Johnny, please visit www.johnnymolloy .com.